MEASURING BUSINESS VALUE OF INFORMATION TECHNOLOGIES

ICIT Research Study Team #2

ICIT PRESS

International Center for Information Technologies
Washington, D.C.

Published in 1988 by ICIT Press
International Center for Information Technologies
2000 M Street, N.W.
Washington, D.C. 20036

Printed in the United States of America

Library of Congress Cataloging in Publication Data
Measuring business value of information technologies / ICIT
Research Study Team #2.
p. cm.
Includes bibliographies and index.
ISBN 0-945098-02-2
1. Business--Data processing--Economic aspects--Evaluation.
2. Information storage and retrieval systems--Business--Evaluation.
3. Information technology--Economic aspects--United States-
-Evaluation. I. ICIT Research Study Team #2.
HF5548.2.M36478 1988
658'.05--dc19 88-8936
CIP

Measuring Business Value of Information Technologies

ICIT Research Study Team #2
Paul A. Strassmann
Paul Berger
E. Burton Swanson
Charles H. Kriebel
and Robert J. Kauffman

Editors
Paul Berger
James G. Kobielus
David E. Sutherland

Contents

Exhibits

Foreword

Measuring the business value of information technologies (IT) is a problem that won't go away. Many are convinced of IT's great potential, yet few seem able to justify or document its benefits to the satisfaction of board members, administrators, and controllers. It's not because we haven't tried. Thousands of determined executives and thoughtful scholars have grappled with the problem.

Executives seem reasonably happy with the measures being applied to investments in general. Accountants busily compile plans and budgets, prepare financial statements, and forecast the discounted-cash-flow returns on capital projects—all according to rules set down by company management, the Financial Accounting Standards Board, the Internal Revenue Service, and other rule makers. Somehow we can't seem to make it work, and our general failure to do so has raised serious doubts about the efficacy of the IT investment. Indeed, our critics taunt us: "What's wrong with you? We measure everything else. Perhaps the benefits aren't really there." Although U.S. expenditures on IT dwarf those of other countries, our nation's relative productivity keeps falling. After years of huge investments, we move from a position of chief creditor in the world to biggest debtor. Perhaps IT has been oversold. Maybe the value isn't there. If it is, why can't we prove it? What are we doing wrong? What does work?

This collection of specially prepared papers offers a fresh view of the problem of measuring IT's business value. The authors provide us with many new perspectives and ideas. They bring both practical and scholarly approaches to the measurement task. Pragmatism and the long view underlie the arguments of the "old hands" at IT management in large organizations: Paul Strassmann and Paul Berger. Strassmann, formerly a Vice President of Systems Applications at Xerox Corporation, argues clearly and convincingly for a new set of metrics centered around the concept of Return-on-Management™ (a registered trademark of Strassmann, Inc.) and shows why ROM should be used as a surrogate for the measurement of business value. His analysis fits nicely into Berger's taxonomy for measurements. Berger, the former Director of Strategic IT Planning at RCA and a long-time student of business-value measurement, has distilled his observations and experience into a compelling argument for using existing measures already familiar to managers.

As we might expect, the ideas of the academicians—Professors Charles Kriebel and Robert Kauffman of Carnegie Mellon University and E. Burton Swanson from UCLA—tend toward theory and analytic constructs. Kriebel and collaborator Robert J. Kauffman describe Data Envelopment Analysis (DEA) and discuss how it can be used to measure the contribution of existing technology to both revenue generation and cost savings. They also show how DEA attributes business value to new technology by breaking apart both effectiveness and efficiency parameters. Swanson uses the power of "idea-processing" software to illustrate how the organizational evaluation of IT investments might be carried out.

This book is not the final word on the subject. Debates over IT's value will continue. Justifications of IT investments will still be prepared and challenged. Measurements will be taken, reported, and debated. Models, schemas, and frameworks will be posited, tested, and refined. But for those managers who must actually do these things, this book offers comfort, inspiration, and, most important, direction.

Brandt R. Allen
The James C. Wheat Professor
at the Colgate Darden Graduate
Business School at the
University of Virginia

Preface

Companies today spend a substantial portion of their annual budgets on information technologies (IT), yet most are unsure about how to measure the full business value of this major expenditure. The sheer magnitude of today's IT investment and the competitive stakes involved have made the measurement issue all the more urgent.

Information technology is a force in the corporate world. Top executives realize that these technologies can make or break their enterprises. No organization, however, should commit to major IT projects simply on intuition or faith. Companies must base decisions on solid and acceptable measures of IT's business value.

The International Center for Information Technologies (ICIT) saw a need for breakthrough thinking on the subject of measuring business value, so in March 1987 we put a team of prominent practitioners and scholars to work on the problem. This book presents their findings, drawing on the study team's original research and long experience. Participating in the "Measuring Business Value" study were Paul A. Strassmann, former Vice President of Systems Applications for the Systems Group at Xerox; Paul Berger, former Director of Strategic Information Systems at RCA; Charles H. Kriebel, Professor of Industrial Administration at Carnegie Mellon University; and E. Burton Swanson, Associate Professor of Information Systems at UCLA's Graduate School of Management. Each of them contributed a chapter of the book.

The research study manager was Joyce Elam, Associate Professor at the College of Business at the University of Texas at Austin and the 1987–88 Marvin Bower Visiting Fellow at the Harvard Business School. The book's editorial team consisted of Paul Berger, who supervised; David Sutherland, a faculty member in information systems management at the University of Maryland, Baltimore County; and ICIT researcher James Kobielus, who edited the chapter manuscripts and contributed the book's introduction, chapter prologues, archetypal and real-world cases, and conclusion.

We give special thanks to Charles G. McCaig, Senior Vice President of Information Systems at Mutual Benefit Life Insurance Co., and Gary J.

Biddle, Corporate Vice President of Management Information Services at American Standard Inc. They allowed ICIT researchers to gather data on their companies in connection with the real-world cases presented herein. McCaig and Biddle also made presentations at ICIT's "Measuring Business Value" conference in Washington, D.C., on April 27–28, 1988. ICIT also expresses its appreciation to the unidentified bank featured in the third real-world case study.

The "Measuring Business Value" research project has indeed produced breakthroughs. The synergy between practitioners and scholars has produced concise and innovative guidelines for corporate decision-makers. By providing managers with excellent tools for measuring value-added, it has shifted the focus from cost justification to value-added and strategic justification of IT investments. It has strengthened the intellectual underpinnings of the subject by grounding measurement in a business-case approach to management action. And it has pioneered in the exploration of measurement strategies suited to the particular needs, cultures, and competitive environments of the companies doing the measuring.

Between these covers is a wealth of practical ideas you can apply in your own company. This is the kind of action-oriented research that business needs and to which ICIT is committed.

Peter G.W. Keen
Executive Director
International Center for
Information Technologies

I

Introduction

How can business executives tell good investments from bad ones? Business people face this question every time they consider investing company money, or when they evaluate returns on existing activities. For many business assets, such as real estate and machine tools, there exist well-accepted measures to guide management decision-making. These measures—return on investment, return on assets, net present value—are second nature to most managers.

The essential function of any business-value measurement scheme is, of course, to help managers manage resources. As the nature of the resource changes, so must the measures. In recent decades, the rapid rise of information and information technologies (IT) as a corporate resource has outpaced the ability of managers to assess this resource's full value to the enterprise. Traditional measures such as return-on-investment and return-on-assets have often been pressed into service, but their limitations have become ever more apparent. These familiar yardsticks are designed to measure the "hard," quantitative, monetary impacts of investment decisions, while information technologies, in many instances, deliver benefits that are predominantly "soft" (that is, qualitative, indirect, and diffuse). How does one put a dollar figure on "enhanced reporting capabilities," "improved communications," "tightened coordination," "added flexibility," "expanded access to information," and "better decision-making"? For that matter, how does one measure a "strategic advantage"?

Managers want to know not only how to measure IT's business value but also what precisely is to be measured. Do they capitalize software and data expenditures in addition to hardware costs? Do they concern themselves with measures of information system (IS) department performance?

The growing demand for measures of IT's business value led the International Center for Information Technologies (ICIT) to sponsor a research study bringing together some of the top scholars and thinkers in the field. The project has developed new and useful approaches to business-value measurement and tested these approaches against real-world cases. In addition, the project has upheld the usefulness of traditional approaches to measurement when applied to particular systems and particular applications.

What has emerged from ICIT's research project is an integrated perspective on the measurement of IT's business value. Several conclusions surface repeatedly:

- Companies must have business strategies that include IT as a means for realizing business objectives.
- The performance of IT as a corporate *resource* and IS, as a corporate *organization*, are two separate matters.
- Meaningful performance measures cannot be made without a clear and consistent definition of the IT asset.

- Appropriate measures for IT's business value can be selected once managers clearly identify what it is they are trying to measure.
- Measures must fit the management style and culture of the organization doing the measuring.
- The metrics adopted must be well-understood by business people and tied to specific elements of the firm's business plan.
- New measures can be included within management's measurement portfolio, but they must be acceptable and understandable to management.
- Even the most ingenious business-value metrics are essentially meaningless without well-reasoned business plans that spell out performance criteria and targets.
- A single metric would not be adequate in assessing the full business value of most IT investments.

Guiding the ICIT research team have been three convictions:

- First, that IT deserves special consideration as an investment category, because it is such a pervasive and potentially strategic component of modern business.

  Expenditures on information processing and communications will account for over 7 percent of U.S. gross national product by 1995, according to a 1987 news release from Quantum Consultants, Inc. These expenditures rose 14.6 percent annually from 1975 to 1985, a growth rate that will decline to 8.4 percent in 1985-90 and 6.6 percent in 1990-95. Annual investment in IT now represents about one-third of total corporate capital spending. Spending on high-tech equipment, as a percentage of total capital spending, has nearly tripled since the mid-60s, according to Donald A. Marchand and Forest W. Horton Jr.'s 1986 book *Infotrends: Profiting from Your Information Resources*. Much of that growth is happening outside the IS department, thanks to the boom in end-user computing and distributed departmental information systems. A 1987 Diebold Group survey cited in the June 15, 1987 *Industry Week* magazine finds that information systems expenditures outside IS amount to an average of 50 percent over and above the IS budget.

  Information technology has permeated corporate life. Visionary executives are attempting to harness the IT resource for strategic ends. Companies such as American Airlines and Merrill Lynch have used their IT infrastructure to dominate markets and seize competitive advantage. The workers who plan, design, implement, operate, maintain, and upgrade this infrastructure—IS professionals—represent the fastest-growing segment of the U.S. workforce. According to the September 1, 1987 *Datamation*, personnel costs represent approximately one-half of the total IS costs, and will continue to grow as a percentage of the total IT expenditure. Outside of IS, the capital-intensiveness of information work has risen steadily over the past 20 years while that of production work has leveled off, according to Marchand and Horton.

- The second conviction driving the ICIT research project has been that managers, without suitable performance measures, cannot effectively manage their IT assets.
- Finally, ICIT researchers believe strongly that approaches and techniques for measuring IT's business value feed into the management process and can only be understood in the context of that process.

Measurements feed into the management process in two ways:

- First, measurements help justify new IT systems and applications, or enhancements and upgrades of existing systems. Justifying development of a new IT strategy requires managers to pull together a solid business case addressing strategic imperatives. This case must identify measures and targets that address business goals and objectives.
- Second, measurements enable managers to track and document benefits from existing IT implementations. Even when an IT investment is made primarily on faith or a compelling business logic, as so many are, it must ultimately justify itself through documented business benefits.

When managers articulate IT's value to an enterprise, they have traditionally focused on IT inputs rather than outputs. Their concern has primarily been with financial measures, such as the total IS budget, hardware budgets, or cost overruns on a particular systems project. In addition, companies have tended to judge the performance of IT—as a resource—in terms of the performance of IS, as an organization. Users and managers have been concerned principally with whether a new system is delivered on time, within budget, and in accordance with specifications. These factors are important, of course, but there is more to consider. Attention has to be given to the value of IT outputs. So far business and IT managers have lacked the tools to determine whether an application truly serves the strategic goals of the company.

The principal ICIT researchers on this project, Paul Strassmann, Paul Berger, Robert Kauffman, Charles Kriebel, and E. Burton Swanson, place the spotlight squarely on the business value of IT outputs. They critique established input-oriented measurement schemes and present new approaches that match IT outputs to corporate goals and objectives.

In addition, the researchers emphasize that the test of any good measurement scheme is how well it fits into an existing management planning process. The scheme must help managers to decide which projects and systems to fund and which to reject or cancel. Meaningful measures of the technology's business value cannot be made without a well-defined process for initiating, developing, and evaluating IT investment proposals. An organization must settle on measurement standards and processes suited to its own situation.

What follows is a case study presenting a composite portrait of a typical industrial company. In this fictitious firm, IT is central to corporate strategy. The case study is designed to give readers an understanding of the relationship between management strategy on the use of IT, and the role of measurements in the management process. The case involves readers vicariously in the management process, letting them experience the entire process through the eyes of the CEO. The case also provides a context for interpreting the chapters and real-world cases that follow.

Measuring the IT Payoff Through the Eyes of the Chief Executive Officer

After 30 years in the company, John Johnson, 52, was appointed Chief Executive Officer. He had spent the past seven years as Vice President of Manufacturing and for nine years before that he held the post of chief engineer at the company's massive factory near Baltimore. The company had been consistently profitable for close to two decades, thanks in no small part to Johnson's ability to keep manufacturing costs under control.

Well in advance of his accession to the CEO's post, Johnson attended an executive program at Harvard Business School. His purpose for attending was to supplement his strong engineering and manufacturing background and to transform himself into a more market-driven leader. The management topic that fired his imagination was the use of information technologies (IT)—computers, communications, workstations, software, and databases—for strategic and competitive advantage. He acquainted himself with Harvard's authorities on the subject of strategic IT: Warren

McFarlan, Michael Porter, James Cash, and others. The examples of companies such as Citibank and American Hospital Supply, which secured business advantage via IT, made a deep impression on him. When Johnson finished the executive program, he left with practical ideas he could apply to his own company.

Three weeks after his return, Johnson was appointed CEO, a move that was long expected within the company. As CEO his first action was to meet with the senior management team to review the firm's current situation and future prospects. Johnson called his six VPs into an all-day planning session. The VPs were thoroughly familiar with the firm's competitive and financial status. The major points were as follows:

- The company manufactures and sells consumer products throughout the U.S. and in 22 other countries.
- In the U.S. it sells some product lines directly to medium and large dealers and to wholesalers for distribution to small retailers.
- Internationally, it sells through distributors in Western Europe and South America.
- It has annual worldwide sales of $500 million, growing at a yearly rate of 5.5 percent.
- It tends to be reactive to trends in product design, letting customer demand and competition set the pace.
- Its products can be customized, and the company has accommodated large customers' demands for changes and modifications.

The company's strategic objectives were fairly clear-cut, and Johnson began the meeting by reviewing them:

- To build market share.
- To be a low-cost producer.

- To maintain flexibility in order to respond quickly to market trends and customer demands.
- To provide strong customer service.

Johnson moved down the list, reviewing the company's recent performance and its impact on each of the objectives. He then began to discuss the challenges that lay ahead and the role IT could play. He called on the VPs to get their organizations thinking creatively about business opportunities through IT. His review of the current status of IT within the company showed:

- IT was used most heavily for administrative and record-keeping purposes.
- Most of the company's systems had been built in house and were 10–15 years old.
- Its Midwestern retail outlets had installed a network that enabled them to provide direct debit and other electronic funds-transfer services at the point of sale.
- The company had recently introduced desktop computers, an executive information system, and a voice-mail system into its headquarters.
- A new order-entry and inventory-management system had been completed a year ago and was in production.
- The engineering department was selling component-design software, built and used internally, to customers for their own use.
- One of the company's plants had taken cautious, initial steps to use electronic data interchange for procurement purposes.
- One sales region had submitted a proposal to allow major customers to access the new order-entry systems directly. No action had been taken on this proposal.
- The marketing VP had asked for help in identifying ways to use IT to broaden market penetration.

Johnson lauded these initial efforts to bring IT more integrally into the company's activities and he pledged his full support of more imaginative exploration of strategic applications. He directed the VPs to sound out their organizations for strategic IT applications. He told them to spread the word that new and aggressive IT projects would be looked at with favor at budget time.

In response the VP of Finance pledged his support for more use of strategic IT but questioned whether management could measure IT's business value-added with any degree of precision. The firm had long used measures of cost reduction and cost avoidance to justify IT investments. He requested senior management to consider seriously the problems associated with measuring IT's business value-added. Without hard, quantifiable measures of IT's bottom-line impact, he declared, there would be no clear way of determining whether this new strategy would actually help the company. Johnson acknowledged the finance chief's arguments and offered to work with him to develop management tools for measuring IT's business value.

In the weeks that followed, Johnson took several other actions in support of the new IT strategy:

- He gave a presentation to the Board of Directors to gain their support for his strategy and for the necessary investments that the company would make.
- He appointed a new VP of IS who had just completed three years as head of the company's distribution organization, and who had spent eight years earlier in her career in IS application development. The new IS head had heard Warren McFarlan and had read Peter Keen, Michael Porter, and Charles Wiseman.
- He modified the management compensation plan to reward successful uses of IT.
- He asked each strategic business unit to set up a management task force to find ways to extend existing

systems to accomplish strategic and competitive IT.
- He appointed an executive-level committee to flesh out the strategy and gain support in spreading the word throughout the company.
- He set up off-site strategy and planning sessions for the top 100 managers, where they heard talks by leading academicians and consultants on the strategic use of IT; worked with consultants to develop concepts of creativity and innovation; and heard presentations on the new company strategy from the CEO and his executive council members.

Johnson and the finance chief met weekly to set up a process for measuring the business value of IT. As a tentative first step, the finance chief proposed that staff start collecting data on management value-added attributable to IT. He explained that tracking improvement or deterioration over time would allow senior executives to assess the magnitude of IT's aggregate contribution to management effectiveness and white-collar productivity. He also offered to work with Johnson in reviewing the firm's IT value-measurement techniques on a case-by-case basis. The chief questions to be addressed by such a review would be twofold:

- What do we measure?
- What measurements do we use?

This second question led to four subsidiary questions:

- How do we measure the payoff, if any, from information technologies already in place?
- How do we measure the potential payoff from information technologies in the proposal stage?
- How do we evaluate and compare various IT implementation strategies?

- How do we evaluate the soundness of the business case for an IT system?

These are the questions Johnson asks himself as he reviews existing IT activities and proposals for new IT systems. In the prologues to the next four chapters, readers can follow his thinking as he confronts various issues and difficulties. In each of the chapters, the authors, Strassmann, Berger, Kauffman and Kriebel, and Swanson respectively, present approaches dealing with these and related questions.

By the conclusion of the book, Johnson will not have all the answers regarding business-value measurements, but he will have moved his company towards business-driven uses of IT and he will have clarified the firm's approach to measurement. Most important, he will have fashioned a framework and a process for management to measure the payoff from proposed and existing IT investments.

II

Management Productivity as an IT Measure

What do we measure and what measurements do we use?

As Chief Executive Officer, John Johnson knew exactly what they had to measure: the effectiveness of company management. The company's chief vulnerability, everybody recognized, was its top-heavy management structure. Headquarters was overstaffed. Between the CEO and line operations were five layers of management. Any technology that could flatten the management pyramid would be addressing a key corporate objective: To enhance responsiveness to market changes by speeding the flow of information to and from senior decision-makers.

The company had implemented three technologies aimed at enhancing the productivity of its professional, managerial, and clerical office staffs. These technologies were desktop computers, an executive information system, and a voice-mail system. The effect of the three technologies was not known. Was management's direct access to current business data having the desired effect? Was shortening lines of communication beneficial? How should the company measure these impacts? Johnson had already begun to address this measurement problem when he asked his staff assistants to collect data on management residual value attributable to information technologies (IT). But this was only a start. The company needed other hard, quantifiable measures to decide whether these investments were contributing to organizational responsiveness and, in the final analysis, to the bottom line. Without clear evidence of the impact of IT on management effectiveness, Johnson felt the company would simply have to regard these technologies as part of overhead.

How should we measure the payoff, if any, from these technologies already in place?

In the following chapter, Paul A. Strassmann proposes measuring IT's impact on management effectiveness through a metric called Return-on-Management™ (a registered trademark of Strassmann, Inc.). Analogous to traditional measures such as return-on-investment, Strassmann's ROM uses existing, quantitative data to determine the value added to management by IT. Strassmann also reviews existing approaches to IT valuation, and he critiques traditional measures of bottom-line impact, such as direct-labor cost substitution and return-on-investment. His discussion helps readers to question the utility of any IT business-value metrics currently employed. It also provides managers with a practical means by which they can determine whether IT is helping their professional, managerial, and clerical staff to work more productively.

Paul A. Strassmann
STRASSMANN, Inc., New Canaan, Connecticut

The tone for this chapter has been set succinctly in an internal memorandum of the International Center for Information Technologies: ". . .How to measure the business value of information technologies is one of the most difficult problems management faces in planning for computer investments. Information technology budgets have exploded over the past few years even if other cost elements are flat or even shrinking."[1]

These conclusions are increasingly echoed by executives trying to deal with economic justification of computers. A 1986 survey of 71 chief executive officers from leading U.S. corporations considered information systems (IS) the most difficult corporate staff to manage and the most likely to increase in cost.[2]

A 1987 survey of chief information systems executives and corporate general managers[3] reported that general managers ranked "measuring effectiveness" and the "systems' role and contribution" fourth and fifth respectively among their key issues. Two closely related issues, "strategic planning" and "competitive advantage," ranked first and second. Other IS executives had similar perceptions, except that they ranked the "systems' role and contribution" even higher than did general managers. It is noteworthy that with minor exception, all technology-related issues ranked as less important when compared with a similar survey, this one conducted by Ball and Harris in 1980, and reported in the March 1982 *MIS Quarterly*. A just-completed survey of 120 senior computer executives by Arthur Andersen & Co. found similar reactions.[4] "Translating information technology into competitive advantage" and "measuring and improving effectiveness and productivity" ranked as numbers two and four in a list of top concerns. A report commissioned by the U.K. Department of Trade and Industry placed the question of proper valuation of the benefits of information technology high on its list of unresolved problems: "The main barriers to the further use of information technology are the lack of appropriate cost-benefit techniques."[5]

The need for financial justification of the value of computer investments is also noted by the IBM Corporation: "For senior executives, cost justification of increased use of data processing is crucial. . . . However, less than 20 percent of DP costs today are supported by business-case approaches."[6]

The following, from another IBM publication, summarizes very well the prevailing perception of value:

> The value of data processing is a major concern of senior executives today. Most. . .do not have access to a proven methodology to quantify the value their organizations receive from their use of data processing. This vacuum has been filled, instead, with cost-management rules of thumb. For instance. . .it is traditional to quantify data-processing costs as a percentage of revenue (or total funding in public organizations) with the implication that holding to past percent of revenue would be a good thing.[7]

Questions

The value of information technologies has received mixed reviews. Public opinion ranges from euphoric visions of technology as the means for achieving all social and economic progress, to a despair about its potential misuses. Perhaps information technology—like any machine or any drug—appears in many forms that may have one of a range of consequences. If that is so, then the public needs to know how to tell the difference between either extreme. Any discussion then narrows down to a matter of valuation. As the price per function of computers declines spectacularly, what is the value of information technology that takes precedence over its capabilities.

Current discussions are noteworthy for their lack of economic criteria relevant to investment decision-making. This is evident when a business confronts choices of how, when, and where to invest a considerable share of the scarce cash available for shaping its future. How does one value improving information-handling capabilities as contrasted with purchasing machine tools, engaging in research and development, or investing in new markets? In one overview of the current state of all information-related developments, Donald Marchand and Forest Horton echo the generally accepted view that "no topic is more complex than the one of finding useful ways to measure the value of information. . . . Research in this area is still very limited, and there is substantial disagreement at both the theoretical and the applied levels."[8]

The central thesis of this chapter is that questions of IT's value are settled when one decides how to measure it. The difficult problem is to decide what to measure. Information cannot be eaten. It has no weight. It cannot be shaped into something that can be easily counted. It is useful only after it is perceived by someone's eyes or ears. To add to confusion, all information has the attribute that its final destination— the human brain—

reacts to even absolutely identical messages with completely different responses. The value of information is verifiable only through observation of human actions. By what metric does one scale something as diverse as that?

Both detractors and promoters agree that production of information is unlike production of any other tangible goods. Information does not lend itself to proven pricing, such as when one buys or sells land, labor, or fixed assets. It is also generally agreed that proven payback techniques do not work in computing the value of information. Existing texts in economics, industrial engineering, or financial analysis tell a business manager how to deal with investment decisions relevant to production of tangible goods but give no guidance as to how to generate information in different forms. Discussions about the flow of information are now emphasized only in texts dealing with behavioral questions, such as organizational design, employee motivation, and personnel administration, fields that are notoriously lacking quantitative criteria for making decisions.

Because valuation of information is subjective, one cannot deal with the valuation of every conceivable type of information. Hence, the value of aesthetic, educational, or psychologically beneficial forms of information is beyond the scope of this discussion. For purposes of this chapter, the object of measurement is not information per se but alternative investments in information technologies.

It all comes down to two questions: How does one evaluate whether a particular IT investment proposition is good, bad, or something in between? More important, how does one resolve the conflicts between various claimants for scarce investment resources?

What Does Management Want?

Measuring the business value of information technologies can be stated in terms of what is required, as an expense justification, by the people who decide how much to spend on the technologies. General management wants to measure the impact of information technologies on profit in terms of:

- Existing financial reporting practices
- Established capital project appropriation methods
- Accepted methods of financial planning and budgeting
- Reporting practices about operating performance

What Are the Needs of Systems Management?

Technology managers need help in assessing the value of technology choices for:

- Justification of budgets
- Allocation of developmental priorities

- Evaluation of long-term architectural options
- Planning investments in technology infrastructure
- Control of life-cycle costs throughout the company

Difficulties

Conceptual Problems

A mind schooled in the traditions of the industrial age has problems coping with any value based on the concept of "information," because:

- Goods lose value when consumed, but information appreciates with use;
- Productivity increases with an increase in the quantity of goods produced; increasing the amount of data diminishes the productivity of information workers;
- The marginal cost of goods equals its price, but the marginal cost of making another copy of existing information approaches zero;
- The price of information has no relation to its marginal cost; and
- Cutting a loaf of bread into halves diminishes the value of the loaf, but making copies may not diminish the value of the original.

Numerous articles describe the obstacles in measuring the cost/benefit ratios of information systems investments. However, published works lack prescriptive methods that could benefit an IS manager struggling to justify rising costs. An article by John L. King[9] is characteristic. It identifies the extraordinary complexities of information systems projects because of their long lead times, technical risks, hidden expenses within the user organization, hindrances in limiting the scope of projects, confusion with the evaluations of alternative designs, and the general lack of adequate cost-accounting information about overhead expenses.

One school of thought suggests that the social dimensions of organizations must be fully explored before one can safely conclude anything at all about the value of an information system. Hirschheim and Smithson make this point eloquently in their comprehensive survey of published research papers.[10] They show a polarization between an "objective/rational" approach to valuation as contrasted with a "subjective/political." No one yet knows how to evaluate the vast arenas of unexplored sociopolitical consequences. Nontechnological costs, such as training, reorganization, and work redesign are already a large component of any computer project. One cannot avoid looking at significant social costs, even when, as in this chapter, one restricts the scope only to investments within the confines of a single business.

A paper by M.J. Chick enumerates comprehensively the problems in measuring the value of information.[11] Chick tabulates 12 possible indicators, only 3 of which he considers feasible in any practical sense. Chick is concerned about productivity in the public sector; he notes that in 1981 the estimated total value of computerized decisions by federal agencies, without any human intervention, was $126 billion. He also shows a tabulation of excessive information costs. Chick concludes that research dealing with questions of how to measure the value of automated decision processes is inadequate.

Doubts About the Value of Computer Technology

For the first 30 years of the computer era, circa 1954–1984, U.S. business adopted a favorable view of the value of computerization. While the total economy grew at a compound annual rate of 8.4 percent (from 1965 to 1975) and 9.6 percent (from 1975 to 1985), total computer industry revenues grew 15.9 percent and 11.8 percent respectively.[12] One can easily characterize management's perception of computers, until about 1984, as oriented toward the mechanization of increasing volumes of paperwork. This wave of automation did not create a net displacement of labor, because clerical and secretarial employment kept increasing above the average rate of growth for the entire workforce. Before 1984 management's concerns dealt with the task of making the new technology workable and applicable to routine data-processing chores.

In those first 30 years of the computer era, U.S. public policy makers, with occasional reservations, also held highly favorable opinions on the value of computers. Except for attention to technology-related matters such as standards and potential health hazards, the primary public policy concerns have always focused on matters of potential unemployment and privacy. The most recent National Academy of Sciences report dealing with this matter puts aside the question of whether computerization creates unemployment.[13] The report proves precisely the opposite: despite heavy computerization, new information jobs have grown at a steady pace. The intense congressional concern of the 1970s resulted in a massive but inconclusive inquiry about adverse effects of computers on personal privacy.[14] So far, none of the public policy inquiries has led to a major legislative thrust dealing with the computerization of the economy.

Doubts in the business community about computerization are of recent origin. They coincide with a sharp downturn in the growth rate of the computer industry, from a 28.1 percent growth peak in 1982–84 to 10.3 percent in 1984–85 to a totally unprecedented decline in 1985–86 of 5.0 percent.[15]

What deserves the full attention of both management and public organizations are recent misgivings about the economic value of computerization. This new doubt was best expressed in a cover story in *Fortune* magazine entitled "The Puny Payoff from Office Computers."[16] A headline supporting this article summarized the entire story: "U.S. business has spent hundreds of billions of dollars on computers, but white-collar productivity is no higher than it was in the late sixties. Getting results usually entails changing the way work is done, and that takes time. . . ."

A similar sense of alarm comes from *The New York Times* article "Services Hurt by Technology—Productivity Is Declining."[17] The article states: "Nearly a generation after American technology. . .unleashed new computers. . .executives and employees are discovering that the sophisticated machines often hamper their work."

To understand the meaning of a "puny payoff" and "technology hampering," one has to examine the significance of computer investments. The best source of this information is the economics department of the banking firm of Morgan Stanley.[18] The indicators they report are noteworthy:

- Computers, office equipment, and communications equipment accounted for 32.5 percent of all business capital-equipment expenditures in 1986.[19]
- The above categories accounted for 90.4 percent of all business capital expenditures for "high-tech" equipment in 1986.
- 83.6 percent of all "high-tech" capital stock in place in the U.S. is in the "information sector."[20]

These statistics reveal to what extent computerization has penetrated the U.S. economy, an extent not exceeded by any other country.[21] The high allocation of high-technology capital stock to the information sector also shows that this phenomenon is of a recent origin. The shift of U.S. capital investments from the manufacturing sector to the information sector and from manufacturing-based producers' durables to information-handling equipment has taken place mostly since 1974. What, then, are the consequences of such a major restructuring in the deployment of high-technology resources?

Total productivity of the private non-farm economy peaked in 1974 and has not recovered since. Information-worker productivity in the information sector has steadily declined since 1974. Information-worker productivity in the goods sector[22] has also declined significantly since 1974.

In the period since 1974, production-worker productivity has increased in both the information and the goods sectors. However, because of the higher proportion of information workers, the net effect on national productivity has been unfavorable. The above productivity computations, which most likely understate the declining labor productivity of information workers, are from data by the Bureau of Labor Statistics.[23] The findings suggest some uncomfortable conclusions:

- There is no evidence that massive infusions of information technology, in support of information workers, have generated discernible national gains in productivity.[24]
- The net employment growth in the U.S. in the past decade comes from exceeding the decline in the number of production workers by growth in the number of information workers.
- The above employment trends show that the U.S. is trading a diminished number of productivity-gaining production workers for an increasing number of productivity-losing information workers.
- The recent favorable employment growth among information workers is largely a result of their declining productivity.[25] Thus, the information industry's many self-congratulatory pronouncements about employment trends should be tempered by uneasiness about our living standards.

Another source of doubts about the effectiveness of information technology comes from a study by Touche Ross International.[26] Its findings are significant because they highlight the productivity of perhaps the most intensely computerized industry. The report shows that the operating expenses of the top 50 U.S. banks exceeded revenue growth for the period from 1979 through 1983. During this period the rate of computerization of U.S. banking has proceeded at an accelerating pace.

The conclusions from interviews with senior banking executives were that "technology has had little strategic impact in banking, despite massive investment by the industry. . . ." These executives said that they "are generally disappointed in the return on their technology investment in terms of their inability to use technology to achieve lasting competitive advantages vis-a-vis their competitors." The executives also said that they are unhappy about their failure to achieve expected economic returns through reduced operating costs.

A similar view comes from Europe. According to a recent survey by Butler Cox: "The most senior managers find their systems departments and their personal experiences with information technology unsatisfactory. Their requirements are simple and should easily be met using available technology. There is, however, a high level of disappointment and frustration caused more by problems with people than difficulties with technology."[27]

So far this author has been able to locate only one valid case study about the economic effects of computers dealing with the productivity of individual firms. It involves an examination of 138 wholesalers, some of whom did not use computers, some of whom used computers moderately, and some who had a comprehensive level of computerization.[28] Firms with "no computer" averaged a return of 11.3 percent; firms with medium usage averaged a return of 9.8 percent; firms with heavy usage of computers averaged a return of only 8.8 percent.

A more comprehensive study originates from the Strategic Planning Institute.[29] It shows that there was no discernible correlation between the uses of information technology (in terms of technology costs divided by the value added of the firm) and the firm's return-on-investment. A similar exploration in England[30] arrived at the identical conclusion that the service sector shows "no evidence to support the commonly held view that computerization leads to a reduction in the information workforce. . .and that the relationship between the use of computers and profitability level is significant."

Doubts about the gains from information technology can then be restated as follows:

- To realize increases in the standard of living of any information-based society (e.g., gains in real income per capita), the productivity of information workers must increase.
- Information workers are the most costly expense category in the economy. Unless their productivity increases, it is unlikely that other business investment, technology innovation, or public-policy measures can accomplish the goal of improving national productivity.
- Computer technology is the capital investment with the greatest potential for improving the productivity of information workers.
- The business community needs an answer to the question of why computerization has hitherto not delivered favorable productivity results.

It follows therefore that questions of IT valuation and measurement become a critical agenda topic that calls for urgent resolution.

Findings About Effects of Information Technologies

My own work in exploring the strengths and weaknesses of computerization derives from the techniques of the Strategic Planning Institute of Cambridge, Massachusetts. The Institute has accumulated, since 1972, a comprehensive database with detailed information about 450 companies covering 3,000 individual businesses. The Institute uses these data to explore the relationships between different business characteristics and business results. The objective is to discover patterns that would differentiate and measure the distinctions between "poor" and "excellent" companies. The Institute, in its prodigious collection of research reports, articles, doctoral dissertations, and books,[31] has revealed new insights into the sources of favorable profit performance. The Institute has quantified the relationships between business variables such as market share, capital investments, product quality, product innovation, marketing expenses, R&D costs, and return-on-investment. In many respects the work of the Institute is similar to the pioneering work done in health sciences that led to techniques for discovery of the relationships between smoking, body weight, exposure to environmental hazards, heart disease, and life expectancy.

As the chief information technology executive of the Xerox Corporation during the 1970s, I was responsible for justifying a rapidly growing internal computer technology expense. It became clear that the traditional measures of corporate performance, for example, return-on-assets (ROA), were not appropriate for judging the results of computerization. With management costs of U.S. businesses averaging over 30 percent of the total value-added,[32] the annual expense for managing a business exceeded, at least threefold, the annual costs of assets for supporting the business.

This background led me to measure the value of management information systems by evaluating their effect on the value-added of management.[33] This approach led to a 1984-85 study by the Strategic Planning Institute on Management Productivity of Information Technology (MPIT). The study produced the following findings:

- The level of information technology expense does not directly relate to management productivity. Businesses using large amounts of information technology do not deliver results superior to firms using lesser amounts of information technology.
- If the ratio of management expenses (for example, overhead costs) to value-added is substantially above the average, no amount of computerization will deliver improved productivity. It seems that excessive overhead staffs cannot benefit from computerization without first simplifying their work.
- Companies that are subject to fundamental strategic hardships such as low market share, heavy capitalization, and an inferior product quality cannot remedy these conditions principally through computer-aided management.
- Computers will not make a badly managed business better. The expenses for computerization and the increased rigidity in computer-managed pro-

cedures are likely to accelerate the decline of incompetent management.
- Computers may reduce information-processing costs. However, any paperwork added by new legislation will diminish information-worker productivity, regardless of how efficiently work is carried out.[34]
- Companies most likely to benefit from computer investments are those that have simplified their management, focused on improved quality, reduced their assets, and introduced innovative ways of delivering value-added to customers. Such companies also obtain additional benefits from reduced administrative costs.
- Strategically sound organizations benefit from computers. They have more than twice the amount of computer expense, per capita, than companies with a low level of productivity.

The implications of these findings are clear: automate successes, not failures.

Helping strategic failures through various means such as generic computer investments, office automation, workstations for managers, government subsidies regulating conditions of employment, or any other public-policy measures will not enhance the productivity of information workers. Most likely, it will increase the quantity of work that does not relate in any way to customer needs. Only highly selective applications of information technology have a chance of delivering favorable results.

Methods of Valuation

Theoretical Approaches

A key paper dealing with problems of the value of information addresses theory. In it, author Robert Hilton covers the derivation of a set of theorems and propositions about subjects such as flexibility and information value; the lack of relationship between relative risk aversion and the value of information; and the absence of any connection between wealth and the value of information; none of which are sufficiently defined and not readily measurable. Hilton concludes, "Thus the general results. . .about the value of information, though mostly negative, remind us of the model specificity and meagerness of the general results in this area."[35]

Without an economic theory of information, the best that researchers can do is try to fit the evaluation of management information systems into the mold of approaches that have worked previously in the factory environment. Doctoral dissertations perennially revisit the classical production theory in order to discover new and clever mathematical transformations that would allow numerical handling of information.[36] Even though these efforts meet the prevailing academic requirements that call for an elaborate display of computational prowess, the prospect of applying the Cobb-Douglass function to a computer investment decision is very remote. Such techniques apply only to homogeneous, repetitious, and totally defined systems (such as in materials logistics for industries engaged in mass production). The complexity of applying these models is justified only if one can support a dedicated operations research team in each case.

Another researcher, Niv Ahituv, has written a comprehensive assessment of various approaches toward information system evaluation.[37] In terms of bibliographic coverage, it is perhaps the most complete treatise in this field. The final conclusions are interesting. First, Ahituv concludes that "the issue of information system evaluation suffers from scarce and scattered theoretical background and severe technical problems of measurement." Then he states that "if the measurement problems are at least partly overcome, there are sufficient methods of evaluation." These ideas agree with my own conclusions that theoreticians have generated computational schemes only to find that there are no practical ways of gathering numbers (for example, measurements) to feed the mathematical equations.

Finding a way to classify valuation methods helps in writing about current practices. The overview by Del H. Smith[38] is helpful, because it suggests a practical distinction between traditional methods of valuation (based on industrial-engineering ideas) and the new needs. Accordingly, there are only two major distinctions on how to approach justification:

Traditional business cases:

- Use the same procedures as in buying machine tools;
- Focus on high volume, homogeneous transactions;
- Concern themselves with operational applications;
- Employ a bottoms-up approach and a technique based on unit costs;
- Emphasize cost reduction;
- Adopt a short-term and payback orientation;
- Emphasize justification by analyst;
- Rely on proposals by providers of the tools;
- Apply to routine clerical work.

Strategic methods:

- Use techniques derived from budgeting and planning;
- Apply to new ways of organizing work;
- Are useful where application is not homogeneous;
- Employ a top-down approach;
- Focus on value creation, margins, and marketing;
- Examine long-term and shareholder goals;
- Employ techniques based on profit simulation;

- Call for risk analysis;
- Examine tradeoffs with other resources;
- Apply to the work of professionals and managers.

Reviewing literature in the field, I do not find any examples of the "strategic method," as defined above. The following discussion presents several representative valuation techniques. They can be characterized either as taxonomies or as revised versions of the traditional business approach.

Taxonomies

The most prolific generators of valuation taxonomies come from the Harvard Business School and from the Massachusetts Institute of Technology's Sloan School of Business. The solutions are always portrayed in the form of 2 × 2, 3 × 3, or even larger grids. In each case the grids identify, label, and tabulate unscaled business variables that name a unique category for analyzing a business situation. For instance, Michael Hammer and Glen Mangurian classify value according to three attributes: *efficiency, effectiveness,* and *innovation.* These categories are then arrayed against a dimension defined as impact, broken down into the following classes: *time, geography,* and *relationships.*[39] This arrangement yields nine cells, into which the authors insert prescriptive investment guidelines. For instance, the intersection of *effectiveness* and *relationships* generates the recommended policy of *replicate scarce knowledge.* Such an approach is of value for tutorial and conceptual discussions; however, its use in valuation of specific investment choices can be only inconclusive. The possibility of mapping any complex organization into a space that contains only two unscaled and hard-to-define dimensions is doubtful.

The most recent and most complex scheme for judging benefits of computerization originates from Cyrus Gibson and Michael Hammer.[40] Their scheme classifies *beneficiaries* according to whether they are *individuals, functional units,* or *organizations.* In the other dimension it classifies *benefits* according to their sources: *efficiency, effectiveness,* and *transformation.* Accordingly, an organization attempting *transformation* should attempt doing this via *product innovation.* As an outline of executive discussion, this approach has much to offer as a way of structuring definitions about the goals of computerization. Again, what is lacking is any semblance of quantitative analysis that would permit making tradeoffs between alternative investment choices.

Of all types of classification schemes, the ones associated with stages-of-growth theories are most attractive visually, especially if they are presented on colored slides to audiences looking for simple solutions. A complete cataloguing of this art form is not possible, because it is so widespread in management journals. In general, these grids bear a strong resemblance to astrological charts. One can find a 4 × 5 table arraying strategic information systems situations (that is, *basic, critical, strategic,* and *transitional*) lined up against information technology decisions (for example, *capabilities, planning, management approach, technology,* and *organization*).[41] One can also find a grid with classification of firms as either *embryonic, growth, mature,* or *aging.* If these attributes are plotted against their *competitive positions* (e.g., *dominant, strong, favorable, tenable,* or *weak*) their recommended information systems strategies emerge as circles, with different radii designating relative importance, against a dimensionless grid. Accordingly, a firm with a "favorable" or "tenable" competitive position in a "mature" or "aging" industry would maximize its value from information technology if it invests in "management information systems." This scheme makes similar recommendations on whether a firm should pursue information products, product growth support, or product cost-reduction strategies.[42]

Critical Success Factors

Perhaps the most imaginative of all taxonomies for identifying the value of information is the Critical Success Factors (CSF) method.[43] This method involves comprehensive interviews of key managers to obtain their views about business mission, objectives, and current problems. After the interviews, the managers' opinions are cross-tabulated, compared, and ranked. From a group discussion about the divergence of opinions an agreement about systems investment priorities is expected to emerge. In this way the CSF technique acts as an unstructured value- and benefit-seeking process that is likely to uncover opportunities that a conventional cost/benefit approach would leave hidden. If the group dynamics of the management team are harmonious, cooperative, and constructive, the CSF method is likely to yield a consensus about the value of various projects. The technique will not work, however, if the management team is in a quandary about business goals and how to apply computerization to solve existing problems.

Because it is difficult to project the consequences of information technologies on long-term costs, the programs that may be of greatest value cannot be assigned reliable benefits and risks. The CSF process avoids such confrontations by suggesting a gradual and adaptive approach to implementation. It relies heavily on prototyping and pilot installations before proceeding. In this regard, the technique takes advantage of lessons from the disciplines of organizational learning, adaptive planning, and personal development. This is in contrast to the industrial-engineering approach originating from the strictly quantitative scientific disciplines. The CSF method may be just the right antidote against some of the worst excesses for conceiving accurate, but meaningless, payback numbers obtained from accounting-oriented cost/benefit studies. It does not necessarily follow, however, that CSF's reliance on opinions and group-think may not steer a business into an equally perilous trap.

Close to CSF's behaviorally based approaches on finding the value of information technology are techniques that rely on surveys of user satisfaction to judge the utility of systems. The methods for conducting such evaluations include some of the most perfunctory mail questionnaires without enough statistical control over the reliability of the sample to warrant elaborate statistical techniques for arriving at findings.[44] In rare cases, the survey techniques document in detail their methods for analyzing the reactions of customers of information services.[45]

The most comprehensively documented project on white-collar productivity, the two-year research project of the American Productivity Center, illustrates the overwhelming reliance on survey methods to deal with the questions of the value enhancement achieved among information workers.[46] In the four detailed case studies presented in the project's final report, the measurement of productivity gains relied 11 times on user-satisfaction surveys and only 12 times on physical counts, which are subject to verification.

Apart from intrinsic difficulties in defining a method for calibrating a numerically consistent scale of user satisfaction, surveys do not address the question of value, except perhaps in helping in identification of a perceived absence of value. Thus survey methods are a good auxiliary means for finding out whether there is a malfunction. They cannot detect how new investments should be made in order to create new opportunities.

A variant of the CSF technique is the Strategic Value Analysis method developed by the consulting firm of Arthur D. Little.[47] This method follows a phased and structured approach similar to IBM's Business Systems Planning (BSP) technique, except that it suggests that systems planning should always begin by analysis of the plans of a "strategic business unit," an excellent suggestion. A planning task force then attempts to assign subjective percentage weights to the relative importance of various business objectives. More is not said beyond this generalization, since the book then proceeds to devote almost all pages to information flow analysis that leads to a logical design of a comprehensive, enterprise-wide database. The rationale of value analysis becomes a procedure in which subjectively assigned weights are sequentially multiplied into average numerical scores for ranking priorities. This technique reflects the reductionist thinking where a small number of very large unknowns is chopped up precisely into a large number of small unknowns. There is nothing in this technique that would shed insights on how this relates to the health of the firm, what the risks are, and which scarce resources should be spent.

Traditional Business Methods

One of the most imaginative ideas on how to cope with the intractability of formal cost-justification methods originates with Robert D. Smith.[48] His

Value Analysis Method begins with a prototype system, which enables the analyst to determine quickly what is important to the user. Accordingly, the user can have a fast but incomplete design to experiment with to discover what maximizes the value of the system. Using this multistage and improvised approach is a way of getting around most of the difficult problems of valuation.

Smith should be given credit for describing what perhaps is the most often used approach for imperceptible escalation of systems costs. Incremental funding of partially completed systems is usually well in tune with the capacity of an organization to absorb computerization. From a budgetary standpoint, it makes the pain more tolerable, since the full life-cycle consequences will not surface.

The flaw with the Value Analysis Method is also its strength. Incremental expenditures without a strategic sense of direction are a very risky way of accumulating a large and inflexible cost base. With active involvement by user management, Smith's approach is likely to work well in growing systems applications where the primary objective is to automate labor-intensive tasks. When searching for a competitive and strategic advantage, the Value Analysis Method, more likely than not, will end up in a dead-end of conventional thinking.

Without an established approach to the valuation of information technology, the author also categorizes private and public auditing reports as one potentially acceptable approach to finding out what is going on. However, only government audits are open to examination, and usually only those with unfavorable findings. They provide exceptional insights into management processes associated with establishing the value of computer projects.

For instance, one of the largest nondefense computerization projects ever done in the United States, the $343 million hardware procurement of the Social Security Administration, merited the following report: "We found that these procurements are not justified. It is not clear. . . what needs these procurements would address, what potential mission benefits would result from the acquisitions, or whether alternatives have been adequately analyzed."[49] It is surprising to see such exasperation in view of the Government's thorough work in specifying how requirements analysis, value analysis, and documentation of the entire planning process should be done.[50]

In addition to Value Analysis and audits, all the techniques that originate from an industrial-engineering approach can also be considered traditional methods of analysis. Even though this type of analysis is often documented in articles and manuals,[51] all cases follow the same pattern. They

- Fully account for existing costs;
- Fully account for automated costs;
- Estimate the additional volume of work generated with automation;

- Always define volume in terms of physical units, such as characters typed, pages generated, invoices completed, and so forth.

Value is then defined as the gain in the output/input ratio or as cost elimination. The industrial-engineering approach produces tables that allow entry of a few variables to identify recommended savings.[52] In this format, office-automation equipment is cost-justified in the same way as purchases of electric motors, trucks, or lathes.

A refinement of the industrial-engineering method is the special adaptation to office automation devised by Sassone and Schwartz.[53] Accordingly, the main purpose of computerization is either to eliminate work, or to make possible a shifting of activities from "lower-value" work to "higher-value" work. With a fixed budget for a well-defined office staff, this technique is useful in identifying opportunities for productivity enhancement through a rearrangement of resources. It will not, however, help in the determination of whether the rearranged work needs to be done at all.

To understand industrial-engineering methods better, one must pay attention to the rare article that questions the applicability of this approach. One of the best critiques is Peter M.W. Lay's enumeration of the most frequent shortcomings of the cost/benefit analysis approach.[54] According to Lay, the major problems come from a compulsion to generate seemingly accurate projections without a thorough understanding that many cost and benefit estimates (such as software costs, expected systems performance characteristics, omission of intangibles, total costs of user involvement) are difficult to obtain and thus are poorly accounted for. Lay's critique emphasizes the uncertainty of any systems venture, thus calling for the use of risk-analysis techniques, rather than relying on simple ratios.

I agree with this view. Executives should be shown not only expected values of a computer investment, but also the extent to which there is an exposure to not meeting even minimum financial goals. Any valuation technique should make explicit those elements that could damage the expected outcome. The major difference between factory investments in machines and information systems investments in the office is the inherent unpredictability of a much larger number of variables that may influence the results in the office environment. A much more elaborate and detailed treatment of the perils of cost/benefit methods can also be found in a National Science Foundation research report.[55]

IBM's Techniques— A Traditional Business Method in a New Form

Regardless of what others may offer about valuation of information technology, any concerted program sponsored by IBM would be noteworthy.

The corporation's extensive educational facilities have a pervasive influence on the ways computer purchasers will think about cost justification. An entire generation of information systems managers and consultants have followed the techniques and procedures defined in IBM's Business Systems Planning method.[56] Their BSP is not a method of valuation of information technology, but an orderly, step-by-step procedure for organizing, planning, developing, and installing new computer applications. For well over two decades executives were secure that profitability would be safe by meticulous adherence to BSP.[57]

The recent work of IBM to overcome the valuation gaps in BSP is reflected in an article by Tim Lincoln, who has worried about the economic value of computers for several decades. His important paper "Do Computer Systems Really Pay Off?"[58] describes payoff findings from 170 case studies. The results reported are almost always favorable: 63 percent of the applications under study had a break-even point of fewer than 10 months. Over 90 percent of all the applications had benefits exceeding costs. Eighty percent of all cases had an internal rate of return better than 40 percent, with 60 percent of all applications having the incredibly high internal rate of return of more than 100 percent. For about 6 percent of these, the internal rates of return exceeded 1000 percent. With the median value of the internal rate of return at 190 percent per annum, it is difficult to compare investment opportunities, since most real estate and machine equipment deals are very good if approaching 40 percent returns. No wonder that proponents of computers have given their support to the System Effectiveness Study and Management Endorsement (SESAME) results described by Lincoln.[59]

Before one can accept such unusually high indications of value one needs to examine the assumptions underlying the analysis and the techniques for making the computations. The IBM method is well-documented. The entire thought process, now called the Executive Planning for Data Processing (EPDP) method, is profusely illustrated in a detailed manual.[60] Also published are numerical examples of the actual computation sheets applicable to a case study within the British Aircraft Corporation.[61]

Stripped to its essentials, the EPDP method calls for a comparison of "the costs and benefits of the computer systems with the types of manual system that would probably be introduced if the computer were not available." When a company applies the EPDP approach, its executives are first asked to forget all about computers and think about the number of additional people they would have to employ immediately to do all existing data-processing work with pencils, calculators, typewriters, and book ledgers.

This "replacement-with-manual-system" method implies a view of the world in which:

- All gains are attributable to computer technology;
- All value is calculated based on the costs of the most obsolete technology available, that is, manual methods.[62]

The EPDP method is applicable in situations where adding labor hours is the only alternative to using additional information-technology capital. On an incremental cost basis, the EPDP technique then quantifies the costs of direct labor-cost substitution. The problem with EPDP is that it aspires to be a valuation method applicable to meeting all retrospective and long-term systems-planning needs. It uses a wide range of unique ratios as inputs into a computer model of some complexity to arrive at very precise but potentially misleading evaluations.

The first phase of EPDP deals with an assessment of the workload. It properly calls for an estimate of the growth in physical volume of information. After adjusting revenue for the effects of pricing, one gets a physical-volume growth rate. Since the real physical volume of output of most organizations has not grown much for most manufacturing firms, EPDP introduces the idea of *complexity growth.* For instance, compound complexity growth rates of 8–10 percent per year apply to banks, 5–7 percent growth rates to insurance companies, and so on. To estimate the complexity growth, individual executives—usually heads of functions competing for scarce resources—guess at their growing business complexity.

The EPDP method does not include a technique for validating estimates of complexity growth. It is possible that everyone will have an incentive to overestimate their increasing workload, even though the physical-volume indicators could suggest otherwise. In this way the EPDP could build a strong bias into a model that everybody knows will be used for allocating scarce resources.

As the next step in reducing all projections to a common base, one has to define units of information systems productivity. At this point all projections and estimates of computing power define the amount of work as *effective headcount.* Thus EPDP introduces into all cost and benefit projections the costs of people who do not exist at all. In this manner the EPDP method severs the connection between IS plans and the strategic plans of the firm. *Total headcount* of a firm is then defined simply as actual headcount plus effective headcount. To compound the complexities, the EPDP method introduces as a measure of the value of computers the idea of *replacement headcount,* which is the sum of all effective headcounts.

The difficulty in following the logic of EPDP comes when computer-related costs are converted into effective headcount. To achieve this feat the concept of *average leverage* is suggested. It has several derivations, the most important being the effective headcount realized per unit of DP resource, defined as the number of equivalent CPU hours per month.[63] These computations assume that average leverage is reasonably constant across organizations (illustrated by a pattern in which incremental CPU hours/month are generated as a result of new application development).[64] The EPDP method at least recognizes that the average leverage is not a constant, but declines with time from 2.00 in 1981 to 1.00 in 1986. Through a variety of estimates by application, elaborate and detailed computations are then made to show how CPU hrs/month translate into effective headcount. For instance, it ends up as a productivity multiplier of six, if six hours of strictly manual work is done during a one-hour on-line session with a computer requiring only 0.3 CPU hours/month. Using this reasoning EPDP proceeds to extrapolate the value created, which, not surprisingly, shows that increased complexity justifies additional CPU hrs/month.

Because of its focus on justifying additional CPU hrs/month, this otherwise useful technique bogs down in an introspective view of the economics of information technology. The EPDP method is an example of how computer-aided examination of detailed data can obscure the way information technology may influence business plans. To judge the value of computers requires more than examining synthesized variables (such as complexity growth, effective headcount, average leverage). Value must relate somehow to indicators that deal with matters that are real to operating management, such as profitability, gross margins, capital investment plans, inventory policy, market-share goals, delivery cycles, systems costs, and so forth.[65]

The EPDP method starts with the extrapolation of past manhour-to-CPU ratios. It maintains that the value of continuing past trends is in avoiding the hire of people, whether the computer investments are affordable or not. In this form EPDP is a restatement of factory-manpower planning techniques. It will produce good results if (1) one presumes that the purpose of information technology is to support an expanding workload of information workers, and (2) that the sole objective of those information workers is to complete administrative work as dictated by existing procedures, and at the least possible cost. Where work simplification, work enlargement, reorganization, decentralization, and stimulation of personal initiatives are not an option, EPDP can be seen as an appropriate approach to valuation.

"Value" Techniques—
An Extreme Case of Traditional Methodology

Cost avoidance, as a measure of the value of computers, becomes even more attractive when one ventures into the valuation of avoiding failure and incompetence. Whereas techniques such as EPDP count as benefits people that do not exist, the value technique is ready to cash in on situations where computers take all credit for all gains achieved through better management. The value of the contributions made by competent management is avoided in these computations.

This approach is perhaps best illustrated in an ambitious work[66] that is unique, because it presents more than 60 well-documented and easily understood success stories that claim returns on investment from office automation as high as 830,000 percent.[67] Any computations that arrive at such incredibly high values deserve immediate attention. Perhaps the best way to understand this approach is to trace the reasoning supporting two very profitable investments.

The 830,000 percent return was realized by a business venture that grew from a $5 million start-up in 1980 to a successful $90 million organization in 1985. To quote: ". . .the president of this successful growth company credits market-research data obtained from on-line databases with creating an additional $42 million of value. . . .The searches cost less than $5,000." If one agrees with these assumptions, the arithmetic of arriving at the staggering payoff ratio is irrefutable. However, does it make any sense to assign almost all of the total value gained to a few computerized database searches?

The case in question notes that the basis of the business was the entrepreneurial determination of two medical specialists to start a new business to offer remote electrocardiogram analyses. In this case 80 percent of the total value created was attributed to marketing statistics obtained from a database search. It follows that only 20 percent of the total value of the firm came from the imagination and perseverance of everyone else, including the owners. This does not allow much for the providers of capital, the sources of the technology, the employee team that grew with the fledgling company, and any other contribution the entrepreneurs received from their associates, friends, consultants, and attorneys. These computations also leave little room for the value of cooperation received from hundreds of customers and suppliers, who are essential to growing a new enterprise.

This case also begs the question of the valuation of raw market-research data. To what extent is this information of use only to those entrepreneurs who are ready to understand it and act upon it? We have here an extreme case of what might be called the fallacy of misplaced attribution, which characterizes technology-centered thinking. The old approach to justifying plant machinery[68] always assumed that people enter into the valuation equations only when their manhours are reduced as an offset against increased costs of capital. Any benefits from an investment would be solely and exclusively assigned as caused by the new machine. After all, the objective here was always to improve the return-on-capital.

In another case Meyer and Boone present a 59,900 percent gain derived from the use of a spreadsheet calculation to avoid a $10 million mistake. It appears that a Defense Department accountant accidentally left out this item from a submission to a congressional hearing. A Defense Department official at the hearing called the accountant, "who examined the original spreadsheet and identified the missing item overnight. Because they were able to respond before committee hearings closed, the $10 million was again included. . ." Here "they credit the less than $10,000 personal computer with improving their odds. . .which was worth $6 million."

Counting the correction of an avoidable mistake as savings coming from a personal computer again dramatizes the fallacy of misplaced attribution for arriving at the value of information. The Defense Department representative who calls the accountant gets no credit for questioning the numbers. The accountant who finds the missing item overnight does not seem to contribute to value. The hero of the entire proceedings, to the extent of 60 percent of a $10 million avoidable mistake, is a microcomputer rerunning the error-prone spreadsheet, over and over again.

Observations About New Forms of Traditional Business Analysis

The EPDP and Meyer-Boone techniques deserve our attention because they represent the most pervasive and most commonly misapplied approaches to the valuation of information technologies. The only difference between the examples quoted here and frequently used prevailing business practices is the extent to which management gives credibility to claims about enormously large savings. The internal logic of the arguments does not differ much.

The overemphasis on the role of the technology to the exclusion of everything else is a tendency among managers who are responsible for explaining why they need additional computing resources. Both methods described above are emotionally appealing to anyone whose livelihood depends on increased budgets for information technology. This does not necessarily mean that flagrant commercial motives dictate the choice of methods that are biased in favor of overstating the value of information technology. Purveyors of computers, however, are convinced that technology is central to all progress and to all gains.

The techniques suggested by EPDP and Meyer-Boone generate the highest recorded values of return-on-investment (ROI) from computers. Nothing else in the literature approaches their estimates of profitability. It is safe to assume that their approach represents the most extreme views about the value of computer technology. In the long run the unconstrained uses of these techniques may end up as a disservice to other good computer investments. Not many experienced financial executives can readily accept 1,000 percent or 10,000 percent ROIs as credible financial expectations.[69] It is possible that the skepticism by financial executives about the overstated benefits from computers comes from proposals that show profitability ratios at least 10 times greater than anything observed in the pursuit of realistic business ventures.

This discussion illustrates the strong bias that ascribes all real or potential gains to technology, to the exclusion of any other influences. By assigning value to technology, one can then easily justify buying more of it. For instance, if on-line market-research information "explains" 80 percent of the growth value of a fabulously successful venture, then there should be little objection to buying practically unlimited amounts of additional market research data. Similarly, if a $10,000 personal computer "saves" the Defense Department from a $6,000,000 mistake, all Pentagon accountants should have no trouble justifying elaborate computer equipment.

Based on a highly selective view of gains, anybody with a job of any importance could appropriate for themselves big chunks of "value-added" and thus claim added compensation or resources. By such reasoning, the captain of a Boeing 747 (with crash value, including the lives of passengers, of $0.5 billion) can claim his value to be much more than his salary. The airline mechanic doing preflight maintenance checks on the same airplane could say that his "crash-prevention value" entitles him to much larger compensation than a mechanics' wages. The air traffic controller can then claim a "collision-avoidance value" and so forth. My favorite case of misplaced valuation is the classic exclamation: "A horse, a horse, my kingdom for a horse!" It is unlikely that the groom bringing another mount to King Richard III at the battle of Bosworth would have collected five million pounds sterling, although that was the price the Pope placed on England in A.D. 1485.[70]

Summing up extreme cost exposures is not a legitimate or practical method for computing the investment value of anything. The technique is acceptable only for estimating maximum risks or gains, like estimating insurance coverage to compensate for accidents, fraud, or other malfeasance.

Principles of Valuation

A Historical Perspective

When the Dutch settlers purchased Manhattan in 1626 for $24 worth of beads and some axes, it was the Indians who thought that they got the better deal. After all, there was plenty of land and the rocky island was of little value. If one takes a historical view of what "value" is, one discovers that what is treasured depends very much on the level of economic development. Agricultural society, especially in its feudal form, values land above everything else. Land is a privileged possession of the ruler. Land is the source of all productivity and wealth. Whoever rules owns the land and thus can make priority claims against all other wealth. Labor is not worth much and information is not valuable, because there is only one source for it. The advent of an industrial society is finally assured when land can be freely acquired.

The chief socioeconomic invention of the industrial civilization is the elevation of capital as the primary claimant against all newly created wealth because it is the source of productivity and wealth. Other factors of production, such as land and labor, are subordinated to capital, since they are readily purchased in the marketplace at values approaching their marginal cost. This singular focus on value originating exclusively from capital is also reflected in the generally accepted method for measuring the relative value of businesses. Return-on-investment (ROI) or return-on-assets (ROA) are then the only right criteria for judging the performance of all businesses and the final measure for deciding whether additional capital investments are profitable.

In the first 150 years of the industrial era, little attention was given to "management labor"[71] because it was an insignificant element of expense and much of it was performed directly by the owners of capital. In that era neither management (that is, knowledge work) nor technology was decisive in achieving maximum gains.

Only in the late 1970s did a new era begin, an era in which capital has ceased to be the critical element for achieving gains in productivity and profitability. The value of capital has decreased as it has become easily available on a global scale to anyone at commodity prices. With increasing expenditures for management—which includes technology, marketing, control, and personnel staffs—the costs of management totally dominate the cost structure of businesses.[72] Even more important, capital structure does not determine the profitability or productivity of businesses anymore. Instead, the quality of management becomes decisive. With technology, land, raw materials, and labor easily available on a global scale, management becomes the essential ingredient that accounts for the patterns of failure and the achievements of business success.

Business people should realize that most of the computers are here to serve the needs of information workers, in management positions. Yet the prevailing valuation approach equates computers to plant-machinery investments. This view fails to realize a fundamental contradiction in such a comparison:

- The value of machine-tool investments is to improve returns on capital.
- The value of management information systems is to improve gains realized from managers.

As a result, no valuation method or cost-justification technique originating from the industrial point of view applies to management systems unless one is dealing with routine clerical labor operating in a factory-like environment.[73]

This observation directly influences how one defines the business value of information technologies. The business value will be found in two distinctly different forms:

- If computers reduce the direct costs of production, they are an industrial-age tool for increasing the output of their operators. Their primary payoff comes from increased productivity as a capital investment. The criterion of ROI applies.
- If computers reduce indirect (for example, management) costs, they are an augmentation of the personal faculties of their users. Their primary payoff comes from improving the ways organizations are managed. If "management" is what one is trying to improve, one must find a way to measure the productivity of management.

Productivity is an index of how successfully an organization uses its resources. It is one of the main measures of the value of information used by management. Understanding management productivity and measuring it are prerequisites for analyzing the effect of information technologies. The following discussion uses the idea of "value-added" productivity as a practical method for tracking the elusive evidence of whether computers contribute to organizational performance.

How to Compute Return-on-Management[74]

All measures of productivity use the simple ratio of output/input. The problem here is how to define the output of management. If output can be defined, determining input should be much easier. This chapter defines the output of management as management's "value-added." However, it is not possible to compute the management's value-added directly. As in separation of precious metals from ore and from other alloys, one has to be clever enough to find a process for sequential removal of everything that is easier to isolate first. If one is successful, one ends up with the most precious and difficult item as the residual.

To create any value, management first has to pay its suppliers. Thus the "total value-added" of a firm can be simply and conventionally computed as the difference between net revenues and the payments made to everyone providing the firm with raw materials, energy, contract labor, leases, and so forth. A supplier is anyone who invests labor, management, and capital to produce a product that the firm includes in its own output.[75] On this basis, all revenue-related measures such as return-on-sales and MIS expenses as a percentage of revenue are seen as irrelevant. Revenue does not count in the determination of internal productivity, since it includes the costs of resources employed by others.[76]

Total value-added divides into elements that distinguish the contribution of capital from the contribution of labor. To separate labor from capital, one needs to compute the price and the amount of capital employed by the firm. As the first approximation one should always use the published financial statement and multiply the amount of shareholder equity by the risk-adjusted cost of capital.[77] This leaves one with "labor value-added," which explains the contribution generated by all labor employed by the firm.

The problem one needs to solve in the next step is how to uncouple the contribution of management from all labor value-added. Here a departure from classical analysis is necessary: this writer's position is that management is the only contributor to all labor surplus value. Management evaluates the competitive environment, develops business strategies, hires and motivates people, pursues attractive pricing and taxation policies, makes all investment decisions, and creates the environment in which a business can prosper. Thus, "management value-added" is simply everything left after subtracting from labor value-added all the direct operating costs.[78]

A few words of caution are in order here, in view of the very broad definition of what management is. For instance, training and personnel development contribute to management costs. Indirect time, such as participation in meetings and coordination costs, is all chargeable to the overhead expense of managing the business, even if the costs are incurred by shop-floor laborers. The productivity and value of all nonmanagement personnel (defined here as operations labor) is measured by physical counts of the output, and from other proven industrial-age practices. If management succeeds in motivating operations personnel favorably, management value-added will increase because the new attitude ought to translate into quality gains, into market-share improvement, premium prices, lower costs, reduced taxes, and so forth.

The Value of Information Technology, As Applied to Management Systems

Using the elimination process as stated above, one ends up with a tightly defined net management value-added. When divided by the costs of management, this gives an indicator of the total performance of management: Return-on-Management (ROM™)· This index has none of the undesirable attributes of ROI, since it does not get weighed by the imprecisions of asset accounting. Instead, it focuses on the most important impact of information technology: on the value-added by management generated in excess of management's total costs. Management value-added also meets this chapter's initial objective of producing a measure that ties into financial, operating, and planning numbers produced by the traditional financial reporting systems.

Earlier we noted that "questions of IT's value are settled when one decides how to measure it." The ROM™ method, because it derives from established financial accounting and planning practices, produces a workable metric. ROM™ also addresses another concern mentioned earlier: that "the object of measurement is not information per se but alternative investments in information technologies." Acceptance of the ROM™ idea can influence one's approach to planning, justification, and management of information technology projects. In order to help readers to apply this value-added productivity metric, the next section presents assumptions underlying ROM™.[79]

Applying Value-Added Concepts

The Value of Information Technology Is Its Cost

The idea that the value of any machinery is strictly its trade-in market value is essential if any exaggerated payback claims are to be prevented. This view forces one to search for the longest life-cycle of an information technology investment. The investment should be at the lowest possible price for any systems acquisition, regardless of what claims are made about its prospective uses.

All Value Originates from Uses of Information Technology

The expression *all value originates from uses of information technology* is a corollary to the assertions made above. It suggests that one can only assess the value-added of organizations if one can examine the use of alternative resources to achieve results. In such a case, information technology is only one possible choice to be put to use. The valuation of information technology then compares with the process of overall business-unit budgeting and planning, rather than to justification of the purchase of an isolated machine tool.

Value-Added Exists Only If It Is Countable, Preferably in Cash Terms

Ultimately, organizations can extract value only from paying customers. Customers can be satisfied by employing a wide-ranging combination of purchases, assets, labor, or innovation. Therefore, one cannot justify any investment in information technology unless one can show the logic connecting it to increasing either the intake or the outgo of cash. Cost avoidance does not count as value-added if it eliminates something that is of no value to begin with. For instance, reducing the unit cost of totally useless memos because they are produced with text-editing equipment is not a "saving."

Avoiding incompetence is also not a valid claim for creating value-added. For instance, any attempt to substitute technology for catching the errors of an insufficiently trained and demotivated workforce should be questioned.[80] The test of whether the investment in information technology generates net positive cash flow must apply in each case. In this way one can detect whether the investment proposal is just an expensive way of patching fundamental flaws in management systems, which should be fixed anyway, mostly by nontechnological means.

Evaluate the Pervasive Effects of Computer Systems

All the current valuation techniques suffer from a disproportionate emphasis on the costs of computer equipment. My findings show that, on the average, only four percent of the total value of a firm is given to supporting information technology expenses, and only one-quarter of that is for hardware; the other three-quarters are personnel support costs, telecommunications expense, consulting fees, facilities, and so on. The small fraction committed to information technology expense becomes even less significant when contrasted with the total labor costs of management that will use this technology. With management expenses averaging 30 percent of the value-added of firms, the costs of people can easily show a 30-to-1 leverage over the costs of computers.

The right valuation approach in adopting computers has little to do with the choice of the technology itself, except for the way it assists people to be more effective. Any valuation must be systematic in its scope and must include full life-cycle costs, including all the costs external to the technology, with particular emphasis on training, organizational learning, employee turnover, work disruption, deterioration in customer service, and so forth. From an analytic standpoint, this calls for simulating the impact of a system. In such analysis, great care is needed to discount, on a risk-adjusted basis, prospective future cash benefits and costs. In applying such an approach, I find that worthwhile investments in information technology have far-reaching, systemic effects on organizations with more than one-half of the present cash worth of a program in the form of the long-term, residual value on ROM™. This is well beyond the usual five-year planning horizon.

Tie Valuation into Financial and Strategic Planning

Because of the rising doubts about the value delivered by information technologies, a new point of view is emerging. It is that the worth of computers cannot be examined by justifying individual hardware and software purchases. Computer investments cannot be justified by the custodians of these machines—the MIS professionals. In this view the MIS is evolving into a corporate function that concentrates on network management, database integration, R&D, and planning the organization's "information architecture." This is far from the all-encompassing vision of a chief information officer to whom everyone connected with information will report.[81] The reasons for such a shift can be directly traced to issues of valuation and accountability for the benefits of information technologies. According to this view, attributed to John F. Rockart, "Only the line manager and his staff fully understand the business and are therefore in the best position to spot the opportunities for the biggest paybacks of computer automation. . . .Line management will worry about doing the right things, while MIS will worry about doing it right."[82]

These are precisely the same conclusions I arrived at through exposure to the financial-planning aspects of diverse businesses. Only after several yearly cycles of observing how actual results compare to plans can one grasp the enormous difficulty within which operating management must balance multiple conflicting goals. This balancing process is a daily and even hourly act, but it always culminates when commitments must be made to ways of deploying discretionary resources. The financial and strategic planning processes are the only practical arenas where questions of IT value can be judged with full knowledge about the consequences on the firm's performance. Only those players who participate in making the tradeoffs in the financial and strategic planning process have the knowledge and the accountability to evaluate how information technology can be applied.

The view from the financial and strategic-planning perspective is then the appropriate one. From there all major investment decisions about information technology should be made. It follows, then, that unless the proposals for IT investments are in the format and language of the corporate planning processes, one cannot expect that they will harmonize with the mainstream of management thinking. Stating it more simply, unless the corporate planning process includes information technology in an explicit way, the cost of information technology is seen as just another overhead cost burden to be kept at a minimum. How to increase the value derived from information technologies can also be seen as a management issue. Which planning method is appropriate? In what form can customary planning questions (such as dealing with markets, competition, products, manufacturing capacity, human resources) be restated so that the value of information technology is included?[83]

As can be expected, Peter F. Drucker summarizes it very well when he points out the need for an all-encompassing view before one can judge the value of automation. "Top managements and boards are right in refusing to make the large capital investments. . .simply because automation is 'advanced.' Top managements are right in insisting on some measurement of the expected benefits, some estimate of the return on the investment in automation. These benefits are not intangible and have not to be taken on faith. The cost of poor quality and downtime can be dug out. Determining what additional revenues automation might make possible requires a. . .market study."[84]

Make Sure to Set the Right Scope for Evaluations

Much of the difficulty in the evaluation of computer investments is self-induced. Usually, the group that provides computer services comes up with the justification of an investment. This approach originates in the industrial tradition that a new technology can be justified only by those who have the technical expertise to come up with credible financial calculations. We encounter this view when frustrated systems managers call for advice on how to deal with a pending proposal.[85] If the proposed investment fits into a factory-like environment, such as a data center, the traditional approach of justification by the provider of the technology will work. Most of the new difficulties with cost-justification, however, concern distributed computer facilities, such as departmental and personal devices. Only the manager responsible for that expense can determine the value of such an investment, because he must explain how the employees' worth will increase. This can be done best at budget time when all tradeoffs in the use of resources are open to questions. It then follows that any personal workstation is an extension of the capacity of an individual to do work. The value of a personal computer is inseparable from justifying all costs associated with employing the person at all.

Competitive Evaluation

Any claim to productivity gains from computerization should be checked against an external yardstick of performance. If a dismal operation improves by 50 percent—which is impressive—the gain may still be unacceptable if the improved operations still continues lagging behind all competitors.

This point is best illustrated by one of the rare cases where good data are available about the difference between equivalent U.S. and Japanese factories.[86] The comparison shows the Japanese company with only 100 workers delivering the identical output as a U.S. company with 194 workers. A closer examination shows manufacturing overhead as the biggest disadvantage. In this category the U.S. requires 64 workers to Japan's 22. This explains 47 percent of the headcount difference and most likely well over 60 percent of the cost difference. Because employees in the "overhead" category are information workers, how does one assess the potential value of an information technology investment to improve competitiveness in this case?

A typical systems proposal, isolated from any external knowledge, would recommend state-of-the-art automation aids for the staff employed as manufacturing overhead. The proposal would focus on lowering the unit costs of purchasing, planning, materials requirement, dispatching, and scheduling. To reduce the initial computer installation costs, the American firm would purchase one of the popular integrated-manufacturing planning systems. The value of such a system would then be specified in great detail. The proposal then would show a significant long-term reduction in administrative expense on the presumption that the new system would accommodate future growth with very little incremental headcount.

With good competitive knowledge such a solution would be wrong. The U.S. firm would not be able to increase its volume against the Japanese firm. Without growth, the economically justified computer system would become just another entrenched fixed cost that reduces the firm's flexibility. Based on a competitive benchmark, the correct information policy for the U.S. firm would be to forget temporarily about computers and invest its energies into finding new ways of running the company. In this case, manufacturing planning systems make sense only after doing away with most of the firm's burdensome administrative practices.

Many claims about the value of computers would not be complete without some form of competitive evaluation. The main advantage of measurements based on ROM™ is that these measurements are good indicators of performance, suitable for comparisons against a cross-sectional database such as that defined by Product Impact of Marketing Strategies (PIMS).[87] Without first screening the marketing, financial, personnel, and overhead costs of a firm for signs of a major misalignment, one risks that internal measurements by themselves will suggest IT programs that pursue irrelevant gains.

Summary and Recommendations

Actions for Business Organizations

A business organization can take a number of steps to improve its approach to valuation.

- Transfer the accountability for investment justification from the providers of computer services to its beneficiaries.
- Assign to IS personnel the responsibility to plan and design an underlying telecommunications and database infrastructure that will give the business the lowest costs for installing individual applications.
- Apply the ROM™ measure to all evaluations of IT investments.
- Shift from project-by-project examination of investments to integration with the budgeting and long-range planning processes.

- Equip managers with analytic tools that will help them explore alternative uses of computers.
- Focus computer applications on improving management productivity.
- Use computer projects to achieve a significant reduction in management costs as compared with the total value-added of the business.
- Make sure that a competitive assessment is used to allocate investment priorities.

Actions for the Public Sector[88]

If productivity growth among information workers is the key to future economic growth and employment, it should be public policy to invest in a microeconomic assessment of the value-added generated by the information sector of the economy. This work should not be seen as another one-shot study ending up in a report. Instead, conceive this effort as a continuing diagnostic program to analyze causes that contribute to favorable effects of information technology.

A research organization should collect from a representative sample of businesses comprehensive data that can identify characteristics associated with superior productivity of information workers. To carry out such a program will require an comprehensive collection of microeconomic information.[89]

Involving the government in the evaluation of detailed information has precedents. It has been less than 50 years since the inauguration of programs to evaluate the effects of pharmaceuticals. Assessing the effects of environmental hazards began less than 30 years ago. Recently, monitoring conditions that affect occupational health has become an acceptable federal activity. The analogies to computers can be characterized as follows:

- Information technologies are beginning to have a similar effect on the productivity of our society as pharmaceuticals have on health or insecticides have on ecological balance.
- The methods for dealing with the long-term productivity effects of information technologies may have to borrow from the methods learned about unexpected interactions between pharmacology and health.
- Traditionally disjointed approaches to regulation through legislation, on an isolated case-by-case basis, can upset the delicate balance between easily articulated social concerns and inadequately understood economic consequences.

Isolating the current legislative agenda into discrete topical issues, such as ergonomics, occupational stress, privacy, paperwork reduction, regulatory simplification, transborder dataflow, copyright protection, export control, technological disclosure, work-at-home constraints, literacy, adult education, plant-closing notification, wage structure, procurement policies, and hiring quotas may be an acceptable way of dealing with problems experienced by individual groups. The cumulative effects of each desirable measure on productivity may be totally unpredictable if not adequately understood.[90] Therefore:

- Technology policies that affect computerization of the economy should always be examined in terms of evidence that will increase the productivity of the information workforce, defined in value-added terms.
- Governmental proposals that increase data requirements from the private sector should include a Productivity Impact Statement that shows the total incremental life-cycle costs of the proposed measure.

Notes

Many items listed below come from a comprehensive search of relevant references, supervised by Dr. Joyce J. Elam, Project Manager, Sponsored Research Study #2, of the International Center for Information Technologies.

1. International Center for Information Technologies, "Sponsored Research Study #2—A Project Outline," internal memorandum, March 1987.
2. American Productivity Center and Cresap, McCormick & Paget, *Positioning Corporate Staffs for the 1990s*, privately published by Cresap, McCormick & Paget, Chicago, 1986.
3. James Brancheau and James C. Wetherbe, "Key Issues in Information Systems Management," *MIS Quarterly*, March 1987.
4. Arthur Andersen & Co., *The Changing Shape of MIS*, privately published survey results, Chicago, May 1987.
5. A.T. Kearney, *The Barriers and the Opportunities of Information Technology—A Management Perspective*, The Institute of Administrative Management, The Department of Trade and Industry, London, 1984.
6. IBM Canada, *A Business Case of DP Resources*, Publication G509-2189. The source of the revealing findings that "only 20 percent" of increased uses is justified, in a formal sense, is not given. It is surprising, however, that IBM would make such an assertion. Its 70 percent market share of mainframe computers should place it in a superior position to observe the presence of a businesslike approach to making major investments, in factory-like environments.
7. Del H. Smith, *The Value of Data Processing*, IBM Canada Limited, February 1983. One may wonder why the major beneficiary of the explosive growth in computer expenses becomes critical of the established approaches to procurement of add-on capacity. Perhaps the following quotation (from page 4) provides an insight into IBM's motivation: "The bad news is that the phenomenal delivery rate of value, by data processing. . .has caused DP budgets and headcount to rise faster than almost any other function in the organization. Since DP costs and headcount growth rates are highly visible and easily quantified, as long as value received is left unquantified, it is easily questioned and difficult to defend. As a result the criticism will grow with the size of the DP budget."
8. Donald A. Marchand and Forest W. Horton, Jr., *Infotrends: Profiting from Your Information Resources*, John Wiley & Sons, New York, 1986, p. 212.
9. John L. King, "Cost-Benefit Analysis for Decision Making," *Journal of Systems Management*, May 1980.
10. R. Hirschheim and S. Smithson, "A Critical Analysis Information Systems Evaluation," Oxford Institute of Information Management, Research and Discussion Paper 13, 1986.
11. M.J. Chick, "Information Value and Cost Measures for Use as Management Tools," *Information Executive*, Vol.1, No.2, 1984.
12. Computer and Business Equipment Manufacturers Association *CBEMA Industry Marketing Statistics: The Computer, Business Equipment, Software, and Telecommunications Industry 1960-1995*, Washington, D.C., 1986, Table 2–2. It is noteworthy that the price index for computer industry shipments in the period from 1977 to 1985 declined from 100 percent to 10.4 percent. Thus the effect of increasingly efficient computing power is not adequately reflected in

making relative growth comparisons in GNP terms. (See Table 2–5.)
13. Panel on Technology and Employment, Committee on Science, Engineering, and Public Policy, *Technology and Employment Innovation and Growth in the U.S. Economy,* National Academy Press, Washington, D.C., 1987.
14. Privacy Protection Study Commission, *Personal Privacy in an Information Society,* U.S. Government Printing Office, Washington, D.C., 1977.
15. Stephen Roach, *The New Technology Cycle,* Morgan Stanley Research Memorandum, September 1985. Because all data in this memorandum are in constant-dollar terms, in terms of computing real growth the rate of decline is even more severe than suggested.
16. William Bowen, "The Puny Payoff from Office Computers," *Fortune,* May 26, 1986, p.20.
17. Keith Schneider, "Services Hurt by Technology—Productivity Is Declining," *The New York Times,* June 29, 1987, p. D1.
18. Stephen S. Roach, *The Technology Slump: Dim Prospects from the Bottom,* Economics Perspectives Memorandum, Morgan Stanley Economics Department, New York, March 11, 1987, 14 pp.
19. According to the Computer and Business Equipment Manufacturers Association, the share of computer and business equipment in producers' durables has increased from 36.4 percent (or $37.2 billion) in 1975 to 41.6 percent (or $123.9 billion) in 1985. This is now projected to become 44.2 percent (or $280.5 billion) in 1995. For details see Graph 2–7 in *CBEMA Industry Marketing Statistics: The Computer, Business Equipment, Software, and Telecommunications Industry 1960–1995,* CBEMA, Washington, D.C., 1986.
20. Defined here as the communications, finance, insurance, real estate, services, and wholesale and retail trade industries.
21. Data for reliable international comparisons are lacking. Based on frequent personal experiences with computerization in Japan, this writer ventures to say that Japan's business expenditures for computerization do not approach the U.S. ratio (as a percentage of total business capital expenses). Most importantly, Japan does not allocate its computer investments overwhelmingly to the information sector.
22. The "goods sector" is defined as construction, mining, and manufacturing. For details about definitions see Roach, op. cit.
23. The existing methods for computing productivity in the information sector do not adequately recognize the rapidly increasing costs of capital. According to methods suggested in my book, subtract the contribution of capital costs before arriving at net labor productivity. See Paul A. Strassmann, *Information Payoff,* New York: The Free Press, 1985.
24. It is often argued that the time delay between expenses and benefits is the reason for the short-term decline in productivity. More than 80 percent of any company's information-systems cost is in support of current operations and in maintenance. Less than 20 percent of IT costs can be considered as investments. In the case of hardware investments, that is even less, because new computer equipment is either depreciated or leased. The cumulative size of the invested application software and hardware, estimated to be at least 20 times the size of current annual budget, dwarfs current investment funds by a ratio of about 100 to 1. Consequently, the delay in realizing payoffs from new investments cannot possibly explain the lack of current performance.
25. This conclusion follows from output growth for the period from 1982 through 1986 (see Roach, op. cit.). During this period the output growth in the goods

sector was 18.2 percent and in the information sector 19.1 percent. Their respective employment growth gains were 7.6 percent and 15.1 percent. It should be clear from these ratios that productivity performance of the goods sector is better than that of the information sector because of the former's much slower rate of job creation.
26. Touche Ross International, *The Impact of Technology on Banking*, Touche Ross & Co., New York, 1985.
27. "Why Managers Are Not Making the Most of their Machines," *Financial Times (London)*, December 19, 1986.
28. William L. Crow and Marion G. Sobol, "The Relationship Between Computerization and Performance," *Information & Management Journal*, Elsevier Science Publishers, Vol. 6, 1983.
29. As reported in Strassmann, note 23 above, pp. 159–162. An independent researcher examined the identical database and concluded that "the estimated productivity of information technology capital is rather modest. These estimates show low productivity vis—vis both non-computer capital and R&D capital. This somewhat lackluster performance of information technology is in stark contrast to the technology's well known capabilities." See Gary W. Loveman, *The Productivity of Information Technology Capital: An Econometric Analysis*, Ph.D. dissertation, Department of Economics, Massachusetts Institute of Technology, January 1986.
30. C.S. Yap and G. Walsham, "A Survey of Information Technology in the U.K. Service Sector," *Information and Management Journal*, Elsevier Science Publishers, Vol. 10, 1986.
31. Summarized in Robert D. Buzzell & Bradley T. Gale, *The PIMS Principles—Linking Strategy to Performance*, The Free Press, New York, 1987.
32. Management is defined as all costs associated with planning, coordinating, and administering a business. It roughly approximates the accounting definition of overhead or indirect expenses. Thus it would include not only the payroll costs of executives and managers, but also the expenses for all supporting staffs such as secretarial and clerical labor, office space, outside purchases, etc.
33. Computerization of U.S. factories consumes a small share of computer costs. Based on productivity numbers quoted before, the computerization of manufacturing is not a source of declining productivity. The installation of a factory-floor computer is also much easier to justify, since it is already a machine tool.
34. The examples of added burdens are too many to enumerate. Their effect accumulates as systematic increases in the workload, which result in additions to overhead staff and to the need for computerized processing. For instance, the Tax Reform Act of 1986 requires companies with sales of more than $10 million to record inventory-related expenses such as purchasing, handling, and warehousing, and to add them to the cost of inventory. These capitalized expenses can't be deducted until the inventory is sold. (Also see "New Inventory-Expense Rules Increase Costs at Many Firms," *Wall Street Journal*, June 27, 1987, p. 27 for details.) Based on my experience as a chief information executive, I would estimate the incremental one-time cost for a major corporation to carry out this new tax policy to be more than $0.5 million. Annual costs, including substantial additional computer time, would be at least $100,000 per year because elaborate changes would have to be made to the general ledger, inventory records, purchasing records, etc. In the same way as certain actions by private firms are subject to an Environmental Impact Statement, federal legislative and administrative actions should be subject to a Productivity Impact Statement.

35. Ronald W. Hilton, "The Determinants of Information Value: Synthesizing Some General Results," *Management Science,* Vol. 27., No. 1, 1981.
36. T. Mukhopadhyay, *Evaluation of Management Information Systems: A Microeconomic Approach,* unpublished Ph.D. thesis, Graduate School of Business Administration, University of Michigan, November 1985. This work is noteworthy because it includes a comprehensive overview of the theoretical work done in this field.
37. Niv Ahituv, "A Systematic Approach Toward Assessing the Value of an Information System," *MIS Quarterly,* December 1980.
38. Del H. Smith, op. cit., p. 4.
39. M. Hammer and G.E. Mangurian, "The Changing Value of Communications Technology," *Sloan Management Review,* Vol. 28, No. 2.
40. Cyrus Gibson and Michael Hammer, "The Benefit/Beneficiary Matrix," *The Consultant,* Vol. 3, No. 2.
41. P.E. Giese, "Using Information Technology to Capture Strategic Position," *Management Review,* AMACOM Division of American Management Associations, September 1984.
42. R. F. Hargraves Jr., "Corporate Strategies and DP Tactics," *Datamation,* June 1984. This article is the closest one can get to a modern version of astrology.
43. A.D. Crescenzi and R.H. Reck, "Critical Success Factors: Helping IS Managers Pinpoint Information Needs," *Infosystems,* July 1985.
44. J.E. Bailey and S.W. Pearson, "Development of a Tool for Measuring and Analyzing Computer User Satisfaction," *Management Science,* Vol. 29, No. 5, May 1983.
45. GTE Corporation, *A Method for Measuring the Quality of Staff and Service Organizations,* 1986.
46. American Productivity Center, *White Collar Productivity Improvement,* American Productivity Center, Houston, 1986.
47. A detailed manual describing this technique has just been published. See Robert M. Curtice, *Strategic Value Analysis—A Modern Approach to Systems and Data Planning,* Prentice-Hall, Englewood Cliffs, N.J., 1987.
48. Robert D. Smith, "Measuring the Intangible Benefits of Computer-Based Information Systems," *Journal of Systems Management,* September 1983.
49. Warren G. Reed, *Report to the Chairman, Committee on Government Operations, House of Representatives,* United States General Accounting Office, August 8, 1986. After reading this exceedingly critical manual, one is left wondering by what management fiat this project came into being. If the Auditor General of the United States is factual, it is inconceivable how a project of such far-reaching social and political value could be initiated and managed.
50. National Bureau of Standards, *Computer Science and Technology: Guidance on Requirements Analysis for Office Automation Systems,* Special Publication 500–72, U.S. Government Printing Office, Washington, D.C., 1980. This manual shows detailed examples of how studies should be conducted and results presented in terms of life-cycle projections.
51. One of the most detailed procedures of this kind is in *Cost Justifying a Word Processor,* Datapro Research Corporation, Office Systems Development Manual, March 1982.
52. R.C. Oman, "Comparing the Benefits and the Costs of Electric Typewriters and Word Processors," *The Office,* June 1977.
53. P.G. Sassone and A.P. Schwartz, "Cost-Justifying Office Automation," *Datamation,* February 15, 1985.

54. P.M.W. Lay, "Beware of the Cost/Benefit Model for IS Project Evaluation," *Journal of Systems Management*, June 1985.
55. J.L. King and E.L. Schrems, "Cost-Benefit Analysis in Information Systems Development and Operation," *Computing Surveys*, Vol. 10, No 1., March 1978.
56. IBM Corporation, *Application Manual, Business Systems Planning*, IBM Publication GE20-0527-4, 4th Ed., July 1984. The popularity of the BSP technique can be seen in similar but proprietary versions of this method, particularly by consulting firms. By far the most detailed example is Method/1 by Arthur Andersen & Co. and Systems Planning Method by Peat, Marwick & Mitchell.
57. A.L. Lederer and A.G. Putnam, "Connecting Systems Objectives to Business Strategy with BSP," *Information Strategy: The Executive's Journal*, Winter 1986.
58. Tim Lincoln, "Do Computer Systems Really Pay Off?" *Information & Management*, Vol. 11, 1986, pp. 25–34. This article describes results of an application of the SESAME method (Systems Effectiveness Study And Management Endorsement) in 170 cases. This work is a monumental accomplishment. Most likely it is the largest study that applies a consistent analytic method in studying cost-effectiveness of computerization.
59. Tim Lincoln, "Evaluating the Returns from Information Technology," *Management Accounting*, April 1986.
60. D.H. Smith, *The Value of Data Processing*, IBM Canada Limited, Willowdale, Ontario, 1983.
61. IBM Eurocoordination SA, *Computer System Profitability Assessment in Manufacturing*, IBM Publication GE15-6141-0, Paris, February 1979.
62. It is a view that would price all existing automobiles in terms of the equivalent market cost of horses. Accordingly, if a 300 horsepower truck (one horsepower is historically defined as the rate at which a horse can do work; it was defined by James Watt as 33,000 ft.lbs./minute) costs $50,000 and the purchase price of a horse is $3,000, then the immediate benefit of buying the truck would be a staggering $850,000 ($900,000 minus $50,000). At that rate the proud owner of the truck could report to a visiting team from General Motors that he was realizing a payback within 20 days, without even counting the added advantages of avoiding the costs of housing, feeding, grooming, and driving the horses. The fallacy of valuing trucks in terms of unpurchased horses is the same as suggested by the EPDP method. The prospective purchaser of a General Motors truck should compare its value with a Toyota, Ford, and International Harvester equivalent. In a more sophisticated form one could analyze what happened to the owner's total transportation costs as a switch takes place from pack horses, caravans, chartered trucks, railroad delivery, air cargo, minivans, or whatever.
63. Expressed in terms of equivalent IBM models such as the 3090. Perhaps such comparisons were applicable at times where the ratio of CPU hours to other costs was reasonably stable and equivalent. However, with growth of on-line and distributed applications, where more than 75 percent of all CPU cycles are away from the mainframes, the author has doubts whether such a ratio is reliable.
64. This ratio comes from undocumented studies from more than 36 organizations, tracked during a 3–6 year period (see D.H. Smith, note 7 above, p. 26). Having supervised several man-centuries of programming during my career, I find it difficult to believe forecasting of the workload in a data center from programmer man-months.
65. There seems to be an awareness within IBM that dealing with such matters directly may offer a more rewarding avenue to cost justification. This is shown in an excellent paper by Geoff Hogbin, *The Decision to Invest—Cost Justifying*

Information Technology, UK Field Marketing Support Memorandum, 1984.
66. N. Dean Meyer and Mary E. Boone, *The Information Edge*, McGraw-Hill, New York, 1987.
67. Meyer and Boone, note 66 above, Table 4.2. To repeat, it is a one-year 830,000 percent return on investment! This is not an isolated case. Here are some of the more successful cases quoted: 110,000 percent (Table 5.4); 86,000 percent (Table 8.1); 59,900 percent (Table 3.5); 37,500 percent (Table 7.3); 32,000 percent (Table 11.2). With minor exception, all payoffs are 1,000 percent or better. To understand the meaning of a 1,000 percent return, consider the fact that at that rate invested money doubles every 34 days. It is also the profitability of cocaine dealers. Thus $100 invested at the beginning of the year would accumulate to over $1,200 by year-end.
68. E.L. Grant, *Principles of Engineering Economy*, The Ronald Press Company, New York, 1950.
69. The average return-on-equity for the top 50 U.S. industrial companies is only 18 percent, as noted in Ben C. Ball, Jr., "The Mysterious Disappearance of Retained Earnings," *Harvard Business Review*, July-August 1987, p. 61, Exh. III.
70. W. Shakespeare, *Richard III*, V, iv.
71. Defined here in the broadest possible sense as all personnel who are not directly involved in the delivery of the physical output (that is, goods or services) to customers. Accordingly, this includes not only executives, managers, and administrators, but also all their professional and clerical support staffs and all purchased services that do work complementing internal management tasks.
72. In the sample of companies participating in the MPIT program, annual capital costs were less than 1/3 of management costs.
73. Where computers or robots are used as factory devices, this distinction also applies.
74. Return-on-Management™ is a registered Trademark of Strassmann, Inc.
75. Taxes are seen here as a special case of supplier expense. All management has some degree of control over its costs of taxation based on choices of businesses, geographic location, ability to take advantage of subsidies, and tax allowances. To measure total productivity of management, one cannot exclude taxes from its cost base. Treating government as a supplier with power to extract a priority claim on total value- added places its role in the right analytic perspective. Because government claims a large share of the value-added of any business, only after-tax measurements of productivity should be used in the valuation of any information-technology investment.
76. This point is not a quibble. Most consultant surveys express cost data in terms of percentage of revenue, thus making sure that none of the data is comparable. Even within the same industry, companies employ a totally different mix of capital, labor, and purchases. For details, see the author's illustrative data about the cost structure of the food industry in *The Consultant*, Vol. 3, No. 1, p. 6.
77. How this computation is done depends a great deal on the accuracy and consistency of the published financial statement. For instance, if assets are considerably undervalued, one would have to adjust the published data to the breakup value of the firm. If the earnings of the firm are highly volatile, one would have to assume a higher risk adjustment to the cost of equity capital. Whenever in doubt, the author follows the practices outlined in Alfred Rappaport, *Creating Shareholder Value—A New Standard for Business Performance*, The Free Press, New York, 1986.

78. Payroll taxes and benefits that vary with the amount of time worked can be added to the wages to arrive at direct wage costs.
79. Perhaps it was Ian Mitroff who said that the difficulty in most communications are not the stated facts, but the unspoken assumptions.
80. This does not exclude the installation of computerized devices as safety and error-monitoring devices. However, in such situations the economics of justifying the purchase of insurance should apply.
81. For the most passionate proclamation of the need for a master manager of all information resources, see W.R. Synnott, "Combatting Corporate Chaos: Why Companies Need a CIO," *Management Technology,* May 1985, p. 69.
82. R. Buday, "MIT Professor: MIS Future Lies in Technology, Not Strategy," *Information Week,* June 23, 1986.
83. It is interesting to note that research on this topic ranked the need to adopt a planning method as the topmost concern of top and middle MIS managers, according to Albert L. Lederer and Aubrey L. Mendelow, "Issues in Information Systems Planning," *Information & Management Journal,* Vol. 10, 1986.
84. Peter F. Drucker, "Automation Payoffs Are Real," *Wall Street Journal,* September 20, 1985, editorial page.
85. While writing this paper I received from a client this message: ". . .Currently I am involved in a project to develop a plan for the use of remote professional workstations in the homes of selected employees. In addition to an expensive hardware configuration (estimated to cost more than $15,000 per station because of graphics capabilities), we see the need for adding to our support staff to help in the installation, training, and troubleshooting efforts. The question keeps arising: What are the actual benefits/savings using a remote workstation and do they outweigh the costs involved? If you know how to complete such a justification, please let me know by electronic mail, because we would like to proceed but now need the numbers to support it."
86. R. Jaikumar, "Postindustrial Manufacturing," *Harvard Business Review,* November-December 1986.
87. See Robert D. Buzzell and Bradley T. Gale, op. cit.
88. Some of the text and recommendations are from the author's testimony on "Productivity of Information Workers and Computerization," in *The Effects of Technological Change on the Labor Force: Hearings Before the Technology Policy Task Force, Committee on Science, Space, and Technology, U.S. House of Representatives,* July 1, 1987.
89. The matter of preserving the confidentiality of detailed business information is amenable to proven solutions.
90. The rising tide of regulation can best be understood by counting the number of pages in the *Code of Federal Regulations.* This 50-volume compendium contains the rules governing private and public enterprises. It continues to grow, despite regulatory-reform programs initiated by four successive presidential administrations, as noted in *Best of Business Quarterly,* June 1987, p. 79. According to the Regulatory Information Service Center, the total number of pages of regulations was 16,502 in 1954; 31,584 in 1964; 67,960 in 1974; and 111,830 in 1984. This expansion results roughly in a doubling in the physical volume of regulations every 10 years. One of the objectives of research about the regulatory costs would be to find out how many hours of administrative, legal, and processing time are needed per 100 pages of regulations.

III

Selecting Enterprise-Level Measures of IT Value

What do we measure and what measurements do we use?

John Johnson, our mythical CEO, asked the new Vice President of Information Services to join him and the Vice President of Finance in establishing a measurement process. When they met, the VP of IS proposed that the criteria for measuring an IT system's value should vary with the nature of its application. For example, systems with purely internal impacts such as payroll, billing, and accounts payable could be evaluated by some measure of efficiency or cost control. In fact, she noted, these measures were already employed.

At the same time, she said, systems with external impacts would have to be evaluated by different criteria. For example, engineering was selling to customers for their own use component-design software that had been developed and used internally. Manufacturing had piloted an electronic data interchange (EDI) system for procurement in one plant. Sales and distribution had proposed allowing major customers to access the company's new order-entry system directly. The common thread running through all this external IT activity was the idea of the company interfacing directly with suppliers, distributors, and customers through technology. "We can evaluate these systems," she said, "primarily by their impact on key corporate objectives such as building market share and maintaining responsiveness to our customers."

She then indicated that another important category of IT investments was the "enablers," which form the infrastructure needed to implement other applications of technology. "It's not possible," she stated, "to make a direct tie between these activities and specific company business objectives; a direct return cannot be measured." She proposed that "enablers" be treated as a capital asset and amortized, even though this would require something current accounting practices expressly forbade: capitalization of software.

Johnson thought her framework was a good jumping-off point for developing a useful measurement framework for management. The VP of Finance liked her idea of using existing measures where applicable, but he had misgivings about the notion of capitalizing software.

How can we measure the payoff, if any, from technologies already in place or those in the proposal stage?

In the following chapter, Paul Berger proposes measuring the business value of IT systems by categorizing investments according to their business impacts and then matching these activities against business objectives. This approach, says Berger, enables management to select appropriate measurements that can function both as investment criteria and performance indicators. Berger calls his measurement approach an "enterprise-based methodology" because it explicitly focuses on IT's contributions to an enterprise's overall business plan.

Paul Berger
Paul Berger Consulting, Inc., Lawrenceville, N.J.

Business executives recognize that their use of information technology (IT) can go beyond administrative and support applications to achieve strategic and competitive advantages. Consequently, companies are making major investments in the technology. Because few executives fully understand how to measure IT value, many of these investments are based on decision-makers' intuition, not on business analysis.

Currently, measurement of IT's business value is equated with the measurement of information systems (IS) department performance. These IS measures consist mostly of data on budget and headcount control, project schedule compliance, and computer-center service levels. This type of measurement recognizes only part of a company's IT activity and puts heavy emphasis on costs and service levels. A 1986 Diebold Research report[1] indicates that 80 percent of the companies surveyed plan to invest in IT outside the IS department budget. The report also indicates that the amount of non-IS expenditures averages 36 percent of the IS budget for industrial firms and 60 percent of the IS budget for nonindustrial firms. Therefore, using the IS department as the basis for IT measurement does not take into account the company's entire range of IT activities.

Another approach to IT measurement is to focus on productivity gains and cost avoidance in staff and line organizations due to the use of IT. Franz Edelman[2] and Paul Strassmann[3] have made contributions in this area. Many companies measure the contribution of an IS project by computing a return on investment (ROI) based on cost savings or cost avoidance. However this approach only looks at cost reduction, a part of IT activity, and ignores the uses of IT in the marketplace and for strategic purposes.

Nevertheless the search goes on to find answers to some of management's questions about measurement of IT's value. Surveys are conducted regularly by Diebold, Gartner Group, International Data Corporation, INPUT, and others. Richard L. Nolan[4], Brandt Allen[5], and Gerald L. Matlin[6] have written papers and articles on how to manage and measure the IT investment.

The IT value-measurement process described in this chapter gives practical answers to management's search. This process depends on three main preconditions:

- The classification of IT activities into categories to permit selection of the proper measures;
- A broadened definition of the IT asset to include software and data; and
- Identification of the top IS executive as the position responsible for making and reporting IT measurements.

The process also emphasizes the use of simple, familiar measures that are acceptable in business practice.

Outline

This chapter is divided into seven sections. Following this introduction is a background section that covers the question "why measure IT?" It describes and critiques existing IS measurements, and discusses two examples of IS measurement efforts at a major corporation. The third section discusses measurement concepts, laying out a basic premise of this chapter: that IT use must have direct impact on a business process and must be involved with customers, clients, or suppliers to be regarded as producing business value. This section also develops an "enterprise view" of value measurement and discusses the importance of using existing and simple business measures. The fourth section (a) describes the measurement process for new and existing IT efforts based on the categorization of IT activity and (b) furnishes real-world examples of this process. The fifth section defines the IT asset, discusses how this definition can figure into IT value measurements, and sets forth rules for amortization. The sixth section identifies the top IS executive as the person responsible for making IT value measurements and for reporting the results to company management. The conclusion then summarizes the chapter's main points and outlines what additional research is needed.

Terminology

The reader should note that terms central to this chapter's discussion are defined as follows:

- *Business Value.* In this paper a distinction is made between measurements of business value and organizational performance. Business value results from an enterprise's external activities with customers, clients, and suppliers. It is measured by such indicators as profitability, market share, and market size. Organizational performance has to do with meeting deadlines and milestones, operating within a budget, and doing quality work. Obviously, business value and organizational performance are both important to the success of an enterprise and both require measuring, but the measures are different.

- *Enterprise.* An enterprise is a complete business organization with one or more products or services produced and sold. An enterprise supports all business functions, maintains a clearly defined organization and management structure, and is accountable as a profit center. It could be a total corporation in a single industry, such as Digital Equipment Corporation, Aetna, Chemical Bank, or MCI. It could be a subsidiary or division of a multi-industry conglomerate, such as NBC (part of General Electric), Hertz or United Airlines (parts of Allegis), or Ethicon (part of Johnson & Johnson). Also, it could be a division or business unit of a larger organization that is a complete and clearly defined business entity.
- *Infrastructure.* The IT infrastructure is the basic hardware, software, and data for computers and communications upon which other IT work is built. It includes:
  - The communications network and its constituent hardware, software, and data;
  - Centralized mainframes and minicomputers;
  - Terminals and PCs on the network;
  - Operating and management software and data needed to run both the centralized facility and the network;
  - Basic transaction-processing application systems and databases;
  - Basic company databases, both internal and external, that serve as the data source for a number of applications; and
  - The hardware that supports these transaction-processing systems and basic company databases.
- *Information technologies (IT).* IT includes the hardware and software for computing, communications, storage, and graphics and is used in the gathering, processing, storage, transmission, display, and use of information. IT is a resource and a capability. All functions of an enterprise may use IT.
- *Line functions.* These are the functions within an enterprise that have responsibility for manufacturing, marketing, sales, or distribution of its products and services. Engineering would be considered in this category if its products and services are sold externally, but not if its function is internal support only. Personnel, accounting, finance, advertising, and administration are staff functions.
- *Information System (IS).* This term is used to represent the organizations responsible for supplying computer and communications products and services within an enterprise.

Background

Why Measure IT Value?

Consider these questions regarding the need to measure IT value:

- Why focus on IT when other company activities do not get the same attention?
- Why not treat IT as a cost of doing business and lump it in with the overhead?

The answer is that treating IT simply as overhead is not good enough. To not look at IT value ignores three things: the size of IT investments, the effect of extensive use of IT on the conduct of business, and, most important, the potential for IT to reposition a company competitively. This last point, above all others, makes it important not to treat IT as just another cost of doing business. Senior executives cannot make rational decisions about IT investments without understanding the strategic and competitive impacts.

From all that's been said and written on the subject, it's clear that business executives care greatly about IT value measurement. Brandt Allen[7] discusses chargeback systems and examines the differences between treating IS as a cost center and as a profit center. Gerald Matlin[8] raises the question of the value of investments in information systems. The New Jersey chapter of the Society of Information Management devoted its January 1987 meeting to the subject. Executives of IS have sat in on panel discussions of IT value and justification. Furthermore, top executives of major corporations have requested that their IS managers report to them on the subject.

It is misleading to interpret the steady growth in IT investment as either a blank check for future spending or as an indication that high-payoff investments are being made. In fact, many executives are unsure of precisely what they are getting for their money when they invest in IT. One thing the business community is demanding is a framework for identifying possible strategic and competitive impacts.

The reasons for improving the measurement of IT's business value are:

- To help businesses assign priorities to IT investments. There are many options to consider. Any method for weighing the contribution of an IT investment versus its cost and risk could assist in the investment decision process and in priority setting.

- To communicate IT value to business and operating management. It is important for the people who make the decisions and receive the benefit to be able to see what they are getting for their IT investment.
- To help rationalize the allocation of company assets. In any business, there is always competition for company resources. A rational perspective on IT business value could help managers balance IT requirements against competing claims on resources.
- To help management decide on business actions that include IT.
- To demonstrate that IT is part of the mainstream of business activity. Of all the good reasons for measuring IT value, this is the most important. Throughout its history, IT has been looked on as a back-room activity, a curiosity, a mystery, the province of "techies." Improved measurement techniques could point up strategic applications and help IT break free of this back-office ghetto.

Existing IS Performance Measures

Current practice for measuring IT value takes two forms. One deals with control and management of the IS department; the other involves justification of new projects and capital investment in computing and communications equipment.

In the first case, the control and management of the IS department, several processes are part of budget setting and of project selection. As a result they deal less with value and contribution than with authorized spending levels. The six processes involved are:

- Expense and capital-budget setting;
- Headcount authorization;
- Expense chargeback to user organizations;
- Cost-center vs. profit-center status;
- User support for IS work, including both qualitative and quantitative information; and
- Steering committees, oversight committees, and so on.

The second case, the justification process, involves looking at the expected benefits to be derived from a new investment in IT. The justification may take the form of a cost/benefit analysis or a capital-investment analysis with an ROI and possibly an internal rate of return calculated for the project. Benefits, or returns, are expected over the life of the project. The benefits are usually based on actual cost savings or cost avoidance. The frequency of use and the justification format followed vary from company to company. At RCA, a cost/benefit analysis including the computation of an ROI was only used when a capital expenditure was involved; other IS projects, those not involving capital expenditures, did not need this type of analysis.

Critique of Current IS Measures

The meaning and intention of current IS measurement processes are discussed below. Where appropriate, opportunities to insert measurement of IT business value into the process will be identified.

Of the six processes outlined above, the first two—expense and capital budget setting and headcount authorization—are part of a company's normal budgeting process. Typically budgeting includes accomplishments during past budget periods plus plans for projects for the coming period. The focus is on supporting the proposals for budget and headcount. The presentation of accomplishments is done to prove the worth of the IS organization; consequently, the inclusion of measurements of IT business value and contribution would be a valuable addition to the presentation. Such measures are not included, however, because an understanding of how to develop them does not exist.

The third and fourth processes cited above—expense chargeback to user organizations and cost-center vs. profit-center status—deal with the allocation of IS costs throughout a company. If the transfer of costs to benefiting departments is based on actual usage, then the products and services sold by the company properly include IT cost. This permits better measurement of return for those products and services. If the transfer is based on an artificial allocation formula, then it would be better to treat IS costs as company overhead. In any event, these two processes do not deal with the measurement of IT business value, but they may give some information on performance and management of the IS department.

The fifth process cited above—user support for IS work—is a potentially useful way to gather business-value measurement data. If a line user organization includes IT as part of the way it deals with customers or suppliers, or if it includes IT as part of the product or service offered for sale, then the line organization can include business measures of IT as part of its own measurement process. If the use of IT is for internal or support purposes only, the user department's statement of support, qualitative or quantitative, deals with IS department performance. In either event, the user department can work with the IS department head to prepare measurements of IT business value and IS department performance.

We should note that events do not happen this way frequently. Most IS heads view their organization as the supplier of a service to other parts of the company; the measure of their accomplishment is the delivery of this service on time, correctly, and within budget constraints. The IS heads reason that since the user departments are the beneficiaries, statements of business value of IS should be left to the user departments to make. The users frequently state the contribution of IT in terms of the IS department's ability to meet commitments and provide continued support. Users admit the dependence they have on this support, but they are reluctant to make statements about productivity or other gains that will lead either to reductions in their budgets and headcount or to changes in their organizational structure. Matlin[9] points out that managers are not willing to assign dollar values to the benefits of IT because "their feet may be held to the fire." Matlin further states: "The end result. . .is to deny the tangible benefit while at the same time supporting the expenditure of money."

The sixth process cited above—steering and oversight committees—deals with a number of areas of IS management. In some companies these committees set strategy and policy. Others are used for project selection and priority setting. Most of these committees deal with the allocation of IS resources. Having a way to measure IT's business value would be an aid to a committee in carrying out its responsibilities.

To summarize, the proper characterization of the current set of processes for managing and measuring IS is that they are, at best, a way to measure the performance of the IS department and their usefulness should be evaluated in that context. These processes do not deal with business value. If the only use of IT is for internal support of other company functions and organizations and the only source of IT activity is the IS department, then these processes are suitable. However, if the company uses IT strategically and to gain competitive advantage, then the budget process and steering and oversight committees could serve as the forums for presenting reports on measurements of IT business value. To accomplish that, the processes would have to be revised to take an enterprise view of the use of IT rather than focus on the IS organization.

Examples of IT Measurements

How do actual firms justify and track investments in IT?

Descriptions of two measurement projects at a major Fortune 500 industrial firm follow. One was very successful and received recognition and professional acclaim. The other was in the early stages of implementation and had not reached a conclusion. Both examples have provided experience, insight, and information that has led to the method for IT measurement that is proposed in this chapter. Both descriptions will include the background to these efforts, the measurement approach taken, the results achieved, the conclusion, lessons learned, and inferences made for the future.

Example One[10]

A major industrial firm embarked on a project to build a human resources (HR) information system to be used at all locations. This system would provide HR departments with day-to-day transaction-processing functions as well as management decision support. The system was installed in all business units and at corporate staff. The installation spanned a five-year period. Primary objectives for the project were:

- To improve management decision-making through direct access to an enhanced database,
- To manage cost increases, and
- To measure system impact on HR productivity.

The project involved the following five steps:

- Building a system with a standard database to be used by all business units. Standards are maintained for data item names, database structure, data item definitions, and security.
- Providing HR personnel with direct access to the database and tools to use it so that IS people did not have to get involved on a day-to-day basis.
- Providing these users with both standard and ad hoc reporting capabilities.
- Collecting data on the cost of operating the system and the total cost of running the HR departments. This was done during implementation, which took over four years to complete. Department cost data was collected for all HR organizations, both those using the system and those waiting to be brought onto it. The basic mix of work was the same in all departments studied.
- Comparing operating cost data for two groups of HR departments: those using the system and those not yet using it. Both groups started with the same cost, and both had increases in cost during the period studied. Results of the comparisons are shown in Exhibit 1.

Exhibit 1.
Cost of One Unit of Work

Year	Dept. using the system	Dept. not using the system
0	$ 82	$ 82
1	87	103
2	91	130
3	103	130
4	103	128

The cost of a unit of work was defined as the company's annual cost of processing one employee. This included all personnel costs: hiring, salary administration, transfers, benefits, counseling, termination, and overhead loadings. During year four, the departments not on the system were completing implementation; thus, early in year five all departments were on the system. Hence, it was not possible to continue the study further.

The study showed that departments having the system increased unit costs by less than half the amount of the group not using the system: 25.6 percent over four years compared to 56.1 percent. This was a good study, well-constructed and well-documented. It showed that properly conceived and implemented systems provide productivity gains measurable in terms of cost avoidance.

However the ability of this study to measure the business value of IT was distinctly limited. Productivity gains for other functions of a business, however important, still represent indirect effects of IT. Designing a study to make these measurements is difficult to set up and carry out, since the effects of IT can only be measured during a transition period. Once the change is completed, the new level of productivity becomes the norm and is taken for granted, as it should be. The obvious next question is: "What has IT done for us lately?"

The use of IT to carry out business strategy provides opportunities for developing measures that relate directly to business impact. These measures relate to the activity of the executive and operating management and have direct meaning to them. They also rise and fall with the fortunes of the business. IT can have an effect on these fortunes, and should be measured in that context.

The lessons learned from Example One are:

- Well-conceived IT implementations can provide productivity gains.
- Cost avoidance is a measure of productivity gains.
- Staff productivity gains have a second-order effect on business performance.
- Company executives, while appreciative, are only mildly interested in white-collar productivity gains and take them for granted. After all, with the large investments made in technology by most corporations, top management has a right to expect that to happen. Management is more concerned with IT activities that have direct impact on business processes and are measurable in business terms.

Example Two: Measurement of IS Contribution

This example describes the measurement of the business contribution of IS organizations within one large decentralized corporation. The IS organizations of 18 business units participated. This project was a response to management's request for measures of IS's impact.

The process was as follows:

- The top IS manager in each business unit was asked to identify measures of IS's business value to that unit. Once identified, measurements should be made and reported to corporate headquarters.
- The following guidelines were given to each participating IS manager:
  - Managers had complete freedom to select the measurement.
  - The critical success factors for the business should be used as a guide.
  - The measurement could be made of any use of IT either by IS or another part of the company. Thus engineering or manufacturing areas could be included.
  - The measurement should be phrased in business terms.
  - The activity measured could involve many systems or it could be the result of a major systems effort.
  - The measurement should be quantitative, although qualitative statements could be added.
  - The measurement could be expressed in dollars, percentages, or units of work.

This effort was looked on as an experiment with assistance provided by John Henderson of the Massachusetts Institute of Technology's Sloan School of Management. The project was designed to show that IS is more than just a cost center, it is also a contributor to business advancement. Fifty-two applications were reported. The results were as follows:

- The areas identified for measurement varied from single-system application areas to major application areas supported by many systems. All of the systems work that was reported addressed internal business needs. Twenty-two of the fifty-two applications also addressed competitive strategies.
- Most of the measures used were for IS department performance. This was true for those organizations that tied their activities closely to the critical success factors, as well as for those unable to identify their work with business strategies.
- Some measures were not for IS department performance. These included: comparisons against standard industry averages, improved response time to process customer transactions, increased business volumes, on-time business project performance, reduced headcount in user departments, and improved cash flow due to improved monthly billing processing.

The experiment produced one excellent example of IT measurement. It dealt with a business unit in the direct-marketing business that buys all of its standard accounting and administrative systems from outside. The internal IS organization is only involved in applications that have a direct impact on business activities. These include processes that enhance customer relations, improve order taking and fulfillment, tighten inventory control and management, and facilitate analysis of the customer base (the one with the most payoff).

The IS organization built systems to perform a variety of tests and analyses on both current and potential customers. The purpose of the systems is to improve the quality of the customer base in order to yield higher sales per customer and to reduce sales and promotion costs. The goal is to increase profits by getting more sales per customer for less sales cost.

The IS work in this example achieved the goal. The measurements used for this organization included cost reduction in advertising plus cost avoidance in customer service and product distribution.

The company had a high retention of customers and a reduction in direct sales costs as compared to industry standards. The company's IS cost as a percent of sales compared favorably to its competition in the industry. In this case, the comparison of IS budget to sales is valid because the IS funds are spent for support of the marketing efforts and have an impact on the quality of the sales efforts. Comparison of this ratio with like ratios of competitors provides the company with input on the relative efficiency and effectiveness of its IT investments.

The lessons learned from this experiment are as follows:

- The only IS work that can be measured for its business value is the work that impacts business actions directly. This is activity that has impact on customers, suppliers, products, or services. All other work, no matter how good and worthwhile, can be measured only in terms of the performance of the group doing the work.
- Line management did not look on IS as being strategic, nor did IS. As a result, most of the work done by the IS departments could not be considered eligible for business measures.
- The measurement of IT business value must start with a statement of business objectives that include the use of IT. Once this is done, data on which measurements may be made can be collected. This process can be carried out after the fact, but the data collection and the measuring would be more difficult.

Measurement Concepts

Premise for Measuring Business Value

The objective of this chapter is to identify which measures should be used, how to apply them to IT, and who is responsible for doing so. The chapter's premise is that the use of IT must directly impact business activities in order to produce real business value. This means that IT use must have direct impact on company relationships with customers, clients, and suppliers, and also affect business results such as sales, costs, market share, and so forth.

If IT is used only to support other internal functions of a company, then a measurement of IT business value is not possible. For example, work done on a financial reporting system that includes decision-support capabilities will improve the productivity of the finance department and enhance the management process, but a measurement of the system's business value and contribution cannot be made, because its impact is indirect. In this case, the measurements that can be made are performance measures for the department supplying the IT capability and for the finance department. Using IT for strategic and competitive purposes or as a product or service offered for sale makes business measures possible. To build on this premise IT activity is classified into three categories for measurement purposes. This categorizing process draws on the work done to determine how to use IT strategically and for competitive advantage. Once IT activity has been put into the proper categories, then the appropriate measurement techniques can be selected.

Enterprise-Level Measures

The entity for making business measurements, including those for IT, is the business enterprise. Current practice is to focus on IS performance to make measurements of IT use, but that is limited and does not satisfy management's need for measurements of IT business value. In order to accomplish the latter, the business objectives of the enterprise have to be treated as the objects of measurement in the IT measurement process.

The reasons for making these measures for the enterprise as a whole are:

- IT is used in many different departments and functions of the company;
- Responsibility for acquiring and supporting IT is spread throughout the company or to contractors and consultants;
- IT is one of several activities that can be used directly to accomplish a company's business goals and objectives.

The first two reasons are the realities of today's business environment; IT is not the exclusive responsibility of one department, the IS department. Engineering, sales, and customer service departments buy and operate their own systems. Bank product organizations define their own requirements and contract for their own systems acquisitions. The third reason above recognizes that when IT's use changes from one of supporting another function to being a direct participant in helping to implement business strategy, the entity measured has to be the entire enterprise in order to develop the measurements correctly. In this situation, the use of IT is intimately intertwined with business strategy and operations. Therefore the measurements have to be based on the degree of satisfaction of a company's business goals. If IT is a critical element of the strategy, then IT participates in the measurement process along with the other elements. Matlin[11] points out that the performance being measured is the collective performance of the management group to achieve business objectives through the IT investment. This is consistent with enterprise-level measurements. To measure collectively requires standards and measures with an enterprise view, because it is the enterprise's performance that is being measured.

Use of Existing Business Measures

The recipients of business performance reports are the operating and executive management. The measures used in these reports are for all business activities including IT. Over the years, a body of measures has been developed to meet management needs, and in some companies special measures are used due either to the nature of the business activity or to the management style of a top executive. Nevertheless, a basic set of measures has gained acceptance and is used by most companies. These are shown in Exhibit 2.

Developing and reporting measures of IT business performance and contribution are important for the proper business use of IT. Investments

Exhibit 2.
Existing Business Measures (Quantitative)

Activity / Position	Measurement Used
Manufacturing	Cost, variance from standards, reject rate
Procurement	Price paid for purchases, quality, timeliness of delivery
Both of above	Inventory levels (raw material and work-in-progress)
Marketing	Market share, market growth, new markets
Sales	Revenue
Engineering	Cost, time to complete a new design
MIS	Cost, timeliness, accuracy
Staff	Cost
COO/GM	Profit, return-on-assets, return-on-investment
CEO	Stockholder equity growth, earnings per share, return on equity

in IT are substantial and the potential for business advantage is great; thus line management must understand what it is getting for that investment. Some reasons for measuring IT business value are to communicate to management; to aid in planning, resource allocation, and priority setting; and to base IT decision-making and support on a solid business rationale.

To satisfy the above reasons, the IT measurements have to be understood by management. Management has to be capable of comparing IT activities to other activities competing for the same resources.

For example, in vying for company funds many companies' engineering and research organizations hold a stronger position than the IS department, the organization responsible for championing the use of IT. In these companies the engineering and research activities are looked on as making a direct contribution to the creation of products and services; IS is not. Neither the engineering nor the research organization has good measures of business contribution, but the perception of direct impact, especially for engineering, exists. Both engineering and research have an increasing need for and dependence on IT, because the complexity of their work requires greater computing and communications capabilities. If the decision to use IT is made in business terms using existing business measures, then the *prevailing perception of other departments' contributions* will not have as much weight in the decision process, and the decision will be made on the basis of business rationale. To have this happen, the measures used must be understood and applied in the normal course of business. Creating new and special measures defeats this approach.

The following is a description of an actual experience in an industrial firm. It deals with the introduction of new analytical methods and measurements in response to a stated business problem. It is cited here to reinforce the point that for a measurement system to be successful it must use existing and understood business measures.

The business problem was expressed as follows: In order to strike a better balance between manufacturing and marketing planning and performance, better performance measurements needed to be devised. The goal was to reduce the cost of producing and marketing the product. The motivation was the effect of competitive pressures on the price and ultimately the margins of the product. The only way to increase margins was to reduce costs.

The history of cost control and standards for manufacturing was long. As a result a lot of detailed measurement and performance information existed for the manufacturing activity. In response to the business problem, new measurements and standards were developed for the marketing activity; these standards and measurements paralleled the standards developed for manufacturing; they took into consideration price and volume effects. As a result a product went into finished-goods inventory with two standards, one for the cost of producing it and the other for the cost of marketing it. The concept was that each of the major functions of the business would be measured against its own standard.

New statements were prepared to carry this information. They looked different from the regular financial statements used for many years by the company. The new approach was tested on a special project and produced good results. The plan was to introduce the new system into business planning and then follow up with regular collection of data and reporting of actual performance against the new standards. The measurement system was never implemented because the new measures and the new statements were not familiar to the management of the business. Even though the new measurements met the objectives, the existing standards, measurements, and financial statements were so ingrained in the culture of the company that change was difficult.

Use Simple Measures

The measurements that capture attention and are used on an ongoing basis by business and operating management are the simple ones, or at least simple in terms of how they are expressed. A set of measurements that are both complex to develop and complex to express will not gain acceptance and use. In many cases the underlying theory is quite involved, and the effective use of the measurement depends on a good understanding of the fundamentals. The best measures collapse a lot of information into a form that communicates the sense of wellness or sickness of the business activity and, in the case of the latter, can be expanded to supply additional information.

The following two examples are summaries and conclusions based on use of simple measures:

Example 1: A company is in the buy-and-sell business. Inventory is a key variable. The general manager used these measures: inventory turnover, back orders, and inventory holding time. These three measures enabled him to control his business and improve performance. He was measured on profitability and ROA. The inventory was his main asset. The measures were simple, standard, and survived the incumbent's tenure.

Example 2: A company processed and sold food products. The company sold to distributors who received carload shipments and then delivered to retail dealers. The general manager used weekly carload shipments as a single measure, but was measured on profitability, ROA, and ROI.

His measure was simple but not standard and did not survive the incumbent's tenure. The reason for this was that the general manager had built the business and was highly knowledgeable about its details and complexity. The measure was useful to him because it gave him a quick reading of status and he knew where to go to get more information. His successor did not have that kind of background and needed better and more standard measurements.

Summary

To measure IT business value, the following must be true:

- IT must have direct business impact.
- IT measurements must be made at the enterprise level.
- Existing business measures currently used by the company should be used for IT measurements.
- The measures should be simply stated and easily understood.

The Measurement

Categorization of IT Activities

The first step in the process of developing measurements of IT is to classify into categories the types of IT activity. These categories will be used to decide on the kind of measurements to use. In order to categorize, the activities should be looked at broadly. Major application areas and major systems rather than programs or subsystems should be considered. The proposed categorizing below distinguishes between internal or inward-looking and external or outward-looking activities. The purpose is to differentiate between IT activities that can be measured for business value and contribution (outward-looking) and those that cannot (inward-looking). Measures of IT based on business value are only pertinent where the IT activity has a direct impact on a company's contact with customers, clients, or suppliers.

Much has been written on how to identify IT activity for strategic and competitive purposes. To classify IT activity the work done by Porter[12], McFarlan[13], Millar[14], Wiseman[15], Parsons[16], and Notowidigdo[17] will be helpful because the principle category for measuring business value is the outward-looking category dealing with customers, clients, or suppliers. Porter's work deals with the generic approaches to competitive strategy. McFarlan describes a ranking process for allocating resources and setting priorities for IS projects. Millar identifies the five key steps in using information to achieve competitive advantage. Wiseman discusses examples and cases of strategic information systems and IT use for competitive advantage. He also provides guidelines for developing strategic information systems. Parsons provides a multilevel framework for assessing the competitive impact of IT and discusses the application of the three generic strategies: industrywide cost leadership, product/services differentiation, and market or product niche.

Notowidigdo divides information systems investment into two types: internal systems that have direct benefit to the company, and external systems that directly benefit the company's customers.

The methods referred to above provide a rationale for separating IT activity for competitive and strategic purposes from IT activity that is for internal support purposes only. These methods also allow for the inclusion of IT activity outside the IS area, thus contributing to the objective of taking an enterprise view when measuring IT business value.

It is important to note that some IT activity can be placed into more than one category. The same application of IT can serve as an internal support system and for competitive purposes or as a product or service for sale as well. This may have occurred as part of an original plan or later when actual experience demonstrated the added applications. Regardless of the reason, the placement of an activity in more than one category is valid and useful for measurement purposes. In fact the multiple uses of IT are important to recognize when determining IT value.

Most cases of the competitive and strategic use of IT documented by the authors cited above fall into more than one category. Many cases of existing work are being extended from strictly internal use to both internal and external use. This has been accomplished with little or no modification to the existing systems, as documented by Runge[18]. Runge says: "Specifically. . .the vast majority of the systems studied (77 percent) were enabled by basically extending an existing internal information system outside the organization's boundaries and allowing customers to directly access what had previously been a system for internal use only."

Using IT work done earlier as a platform for new competitive applications also makes the point that much of IT work involves asset building. *It is the baseline work and the infrastructure that can be leveraged for broader gains.* Very often the broader use of an application and the resulting gains were not originally envisaged for the investment. This seems to make a strong case for serendipity and opportunism. When management becomes aware of the value of IT, strategy and planning join serendipity and opportunism in finding strategic and competitive uses of IT.

It is important to recognize as a concept the different levels of IT activity. If the basic work of defining an architecture and building an infrastructure is done and put into place, then it is possible to either build new applications on this foundation or to use existing work in new areas. The IT classification method described here and the IT asset concept described later in this chapter are both intended to recognize investments in

- IT asset-building
- Systems that are both inward-looking and outward-looking
- New efforts for outward-looking systems only.

These investments are part of the measurement process. Let us put this into a proper perspective. A company strategy should be enunciated that identifies the infrastructure and baseline building as part of an overall plan to derive the maximum benefits from IT. The strategy and the plan that comes from it should present a clear picture of how management intends to use IT in running the business. Priorities should be set based on the enterprise business strategy, and these priorities should be for all business activities, including the use of IT. Then, based on the clarification of management expectations as expressed in a strategy, a plan, and a set of priorities, standards of measurements can be set to measure business performance against expectations.

Because IT is part of this process, the same measures are used for it. This is done with an explicit recognition of the different nature of IT work: foundation building, internal support, strategic systems use, business analysis, competitive advantage, product or service enhancement, product or service differentiation, and IT products or services. Once this is done, then the appropriate measures can be selected and used.

Categories and Measures

IT activity is classified into three categories using the methods described above. As pointed out, a particular activity can be placed into more than one category. For example, an internal system used for inventory management and automatic purchase-order processing may also be offered for sale outside the company. If so, this system would be both an internal system and a product and should be measured accordingly.

The three categories and associated measures are as follows:

Categories of Activities	**Measures**
1. Internal/Operational	Cost, timeliness, accuracy, quality
2. Strategic/Competitive	Measures used are based on business action such as increased market share, new market penetration, lower product costs
3. Product/Service	ROI, ROA

The following sections expand on these three categories and the measures used for each. The focus of the categorization is to provide a basis for selecting the correct measure to use. Not all of the measures identified for a category will be used by any one company. It is expected that each company, after categorizing the IT activities, will select the measure or measures that are most useful to its management.

Category One: Internal/Operational

The activities in this category are internally focused and are mainly used to support other functions. Category One activities do not directly make an impact on the marketplace, customers, suppliers, products, or services. They are measured by performance of the department producing the systems application, and by the performance, usually improved productivity, of the user departments that benefit from the system. Examples of Category One measures are:

- A company wants to know whether its IS activity is cost-effective, and whether the cost of systems development and computer operations are the lowest possible for the service levels and quality required. The measures used are the costs of providing computer systems, computer services, system support, and so forth; comparisons with past performance; comparisons with national and industry averages; and comparisons with selected peer companies. The focus is on keeping overall and unit costs down. Emphasis is on expense and capital budgets.
- Another basis of measurement is the timeliness of systems development, production runs, response to requests for changes, and new work. The measures used are comparisons of the delivery of completed systems vs. schedules and commitments; the ability to accelerate work schedules in response to business changes; and the ability to correct errors and problems promptly to avoid negative business impact. Emphasis is on meeting schedules and commitments.
- The accuracy of the information produced by information systems is a critical factor in systems performance. Measures used are reduction in the number of restarts and reruns to get correct results as compared to previous experience and good audit reports. Emphasis is on correct data in the databases, right answers in reports, correct statements, bills, checks, etc.
- Quality is the most subjective measurement of this group. It deals with the systems' responsiveness to change and the handling of a broader range of applications than originally specified, human-engineered interfaces, well-designed reports and screens, etc. Quantitative measures of system quality are difficult to develop.

In general, measurement of IT value for activity placed into Category One deals with the cost and performance of providing IT capability for the company. The only two possible views of business impact for IT work in this category are negative and neutral. If the use of IT fails in timeliness or accuracy, then the result can have negative business impact. Take for example bills going out late or incorrect, orders not recorded or not processed, inventory levels miscalculated, or checks prepared incorrectly. The negative business impact is obvious. However, performing these tasks correctly and on time does not add (in terms of business impact) to anything else that was done. Therefore when performing properly, the internal IT activity is neutral when considering business impact.

Organizational performance measures should be developed for the suppliers (both internal to the company and outside the company) of IT capability placed into Category One. This may be done as follows:

- At budget time, set expense and capital budget requirements for the organizations.
- For outside suppliers and consultants, set contract terms for fees based on delivery and adherence to specifications.
- Set departmental goals for adherence to schedules, response time, lost time due to reruns and restarts, and time to correct errors.

Category Two: Strategic/Competitive

The IT activities in Category Two deal with the marketplace, customers, suppliers, products, and services. As such, appropriate company business measures should be used. (For a discussion of industry business strategies and the performance measures associated with them, see Oliva, Day, and DeSarbo.)[19]

In some cases additional data must be collected to be able to perform the measurement. For example, the determination of improved customer image for the company might require market research to collect the data and measure results. Examples of the types of measures used are:

- The company wants to increase market share and using IT can make the difference; it can improve market share by providing better information directly to customers about order status, billings, product availability, price concessions, etc. The measure to use here is the change in market share. If it increases, then the company has succeeded in achieving its goal; the use of IT directly helped in the process.
- The company takes steps to increase sales to existing customers. Through IT, customers are allowed to enter orders directly into the company's order-entry system and to check inventory status and pricing. The company uses IT to analyze the customer's inventory position and order patterns as well as assist customers in managing their inventories and placing orders. The measure is the change in sales revenue from existing customers as compared to company goals.

- A financial services company with an extensive telecommunications network in place decides to create new services and products to sell to existing and new customers. Goals are increased sales revenue, additional customers, and a new market. Measures are the change in revenue and the number of customers compared with company goals.
- Because of competitive pressures, a company wants to improve product design quality and reduce time from concept to start of manufacturing through the use of IT. The measures used are actual design time compared to company goals and the reduction in design rework and engineering change orders once production has started. The latter is compared against previous experience.
- A company wants to reduce inventory and material-handling costs through the use of IT. The company installs a communications network to its suppliers and provides a system to transmit orders, check on quality control, and process order releases. The measures used are lower inventory levels, less cost for materials, and less time lost for rejects.

Questions can be asked about the examples above, such as,

- How can an entire change be treated as the result of IT?
- Couldn't external factors affect the outcome of a company action?
- The measurements in the examples above make comparisons against company business goals. Shouldn't IT investment be the basis of measurement?

Developing measures for IT business value is not akin to the search for the Holy Grail. It is a pragmatic, realistic way to help business people view the value of IT in a business situation. Using IT is not a fad, nor is it an end in itself. The only reason for a company to use IT for competitive or strategic purposes is to accomplish management's goals. If those goals are realized with IT as a necessary, direct, and major part of the business implementation, then IT value would be positive as measured by the positive business accomplishment. If the goals are not realized with IT, a necessary and major part of the implementation, then IT value would be negative as measured by the lack of business accomplishment.

The reason for not reaching business goals should be explored. If the failure is due to actions under control of the company, then corrective actions can be taken. If the failure is due to external situations not under company control, then corrective actions may not be possible. In either case, the business goals of the enterprise were not met and the management did not succeed.

As a separate issue the performance of individual organizations in fulfilling their roles can be measured, including IS. This is useful in determining rewards or blame, future participation, budgets, headcount, and so on. It is also useful in diagnosing problems and taking corrective action.

It is interesting to look at inventive and creative IT work for its own sake, but unless the business reason for its use is successful, it does not have positive business value. It is true that the work developed might have value in another application, but if so, that application should be classified and measured on its own merits. The net result is that the measure of IT value in situations where it is being used for business advantage is the measurement of the business activity in relation to the goals set for it.

The base used to make measurements depends on the project and on management expectations and objectives for it. The investment in IT joins with other activity and organization costs in making up the enterprise's investment. The following discussion provides more detail on this process.

The steps for measurement of IT value in cases where it is used for strategic or competitive purposes are:

- Set company objectives and goals.
- Decide if IT is needed to accomplish them. If information technology is not needed for the business effort, then the next step does not apply and the final step does not include IT.
- Include IT investment in total investment of the project to decide on business viability of the effort. If a company has treated its infrastructure as a capital good, then a portion of the amortization should be included, too.
- Collect data and make measurements of the project to determine progress.
- Measure results against goals set for the project in the first step.
- The degrees to which the goals are reached are a measure of success or failure for the entire effort, including IT.

It is becoming more obvious to company management that the use of IT can make substantive contributions to business endeavors. When Category Two IT activity occurs, then the inclusion of IT investment and IT activity into business measurement fits, and the six steps outlined above should be followed.

Category Three: Product/Service

The activities in Category Three include revenue-producing IT products and services for firms whose principle business is not the production and sale of IT. This is to distinguish vendors of computer and communications hardware and software from firms engaged in other businesses that gain revenue from IT. Obviously the same measures are used. The difference is that IBM, DEC, and others have been involved in measuring their performance from IT since their founding, while banks or insurance companies have not.

An IT activity fits into Category Three when:

- An IT application is developed into a product or service that is being marketed for profit. This may occur when a company discovers that it has developed something for itself that has value in the marketplace, or the company has acquired a product for which there is demand, or a subsidiary is acquired that provides IT products or services. A company that provides IT products or services as value-added to their customers would treat that use of IT as a Category Two activity.
- A separate organization can be identified, at least in an accounting sense. It is necessary to be able to identify assets, liabilities, revenue, costs, profits.

The measurements for Category Three are the standard measures used by a company for any other of its businesses, typically profitability measures. They are return on assets, return on investment, and return on equity.

In some cases where companies try to recover some of the cost of developing a system, they are not in the business of marketing IT for a profit and therefore should use measurements in Categories One or Two. The handling of any recovery that is realized would be determined by the accounting system and have nothing to do with the business value of IT.

Some examples of Category Three use of IT are:

- American Airlines' sale of service on its reservation system to other airlines;
- A bank's sale of cash-management software to all comers;
- A consulting firm's sale of a planning package. Customers for the package may be restricted to clients or not. The test for Category Three above must be met.

Measurements: Process for a New Initiative

In a case where a new business initiative is beginning, the process for developing measures begins with management activity that includes setting company business objectives, business strategy, and business plans. This is the point where decisions are made on how the company will spend its resources and what it expects to get in return for the use of the resources. The degree of formality is not critical. The activity is. A decision on the need for IT to accomplish the objectives can be made at this stage, the first step in the new initiative.

The next step is to select the specific organizations and functions needed to carry out the plan. If in the first step the decision was made to use technology to accomplish the company objectives, then IT is part of the resource allocation and decisions are made here on what organizations are involved with implementation. If the IT decision were not made in the first step, it is made at this one.

Based on the above process, the measurements for IT are treated as follows:

- If IT is not part of the plan, then the subject of IT measurements does not enter into consideration.
- If IT is needed for administrative, record-keeping, or other support activities (Category One), then measures for internal activities should be used.
- If IT is a key ingredient and an agent for the successful implementation of the business plan (Category Two), then the measurements used for the success or failure of the plan are also the measurements for IT.
- If IT is the basis of the new product or service offered to accomplish the company's objectives (Category Three), then the measures used for IT are the company's measures for any new product or service.

The decisions on what to measure and whether to measure IT value are tied directly to the management decision process.

Measurements: Process for Existing IT Efforts

The process for developing measures for existing business uses of IT is as follows:

- Classify existing IT activity into the three categories.
- Use the measurements identified for each category that are consistent with company measurement usage.

In the case of IT activity falling into Category Two, the identification of IT contribution is an important step in itself. The gains or losses of the business activity become the measures for IT, because they are measures of enterprise activity of which IT is a part.

Applying the Measurement Process

An example of how to identify and apply the measurement approach will clarify the steps in the process.

A company initiated a program to change its warehousing and distribution system. It had placed a number of full-service warehouses around the country with the intention of guaranteeing customers product delivery within 48 hours. The inventory and labor costs were high for this system, there were failures to meet the 48-hour delivery commitment, and customers were demanding that certain products be delivered in 24 hours.

A study of the program showed the following:

- Some products were required by customers in 24 hours after ordering or the business would go to competitors who could meet delivery requirements.
- Some products could be delivered in four days to a week to meet customer needs.
- Some products could be delivered within two weeks of ordering without negatively affecting customer attitude or losing sales.

As a result of the study the following plan was proposed:

- Maintain one full-service warehouse in a central location. This warehouse will handle all shipments of products with more than a 24-hour delivery requirement.
- Place a number of "hot" warehouses, those holding only the product with 24-hour delivery requirements, in locations close to dense customer areas.
- Revamp the computer systems to handle the new warehouse configuration, ordering needs, and fulfillment requirements.

The new proposal promised significant cost savings for reduced headcount, reduced warehouse floor space, and lower inventory. It also promised to protect sales to existing customers and projected increased sales from new customers because of better ability to respond to 24-hour delivery needs. The resulting profit improvement was necessary for the continued viability of the business.

To implement the proposal, computer systems had to be changed and new programs added. In fact, operating management stated that the new plan could not be realized without the support and work of the MIS department. All of the computer-systems work was internal (Category One). It was in support of other business activities and departments. The measures used were on-time completion of the systems in a fully operational mode within the budget for the project (timeliness, accuracy, cost). However the IT work was essential to the success of the strategic business change and an argument could be made that this was a strategic use of IT. It was, but not for measurement purposes.

The project was measured by increased profit due to greater sales, lower costs (headcount, space, inventory, shipping), and ROI.

If the new plan had included provision for customers to use the company's computer systems directly to check inventory, to place orders, and to monitor order status, and this was necessary to meet the plan objectives, then the computer-systems work would be classified as both Categories One and Two. The IS department would have been measured the same as above, but IT would be considered a direct part of the new process and be treated as a direct business contribution to the project goals described above. If the plan succeeded, IT would be considered one of the contributing factors to the sales and ROI increase. On the other hand, if the plan did not succeed, then IT would stand with the other involved components of the business as not helping the company achieve its business goals.

One other comment can be made about this example: IT activity classified in Category One cannot be treated as making a direct positive contribution to the accomplishment of the plan objectives. If MIS fails to meet its goals, however, it can have a direct negative impact on the ability of the company to meet its plan objectives.

This is the harsh reality for IS organizations that are only involved with Category One activity: downside risk without commensurate upside payoff. It is true that IS departments that score high on Category One measures (cost, timeliness, accuracy) are given recognition and rewards. In fact some of the best-recognized IS executives lead organizations that exhibit these qualities.

The Information Technology Asset

The IT Asset Concept

The definition of an IT asset that properly considers all long-term investments, including software and data, is essential to developing IT measurements. In developing IT measurements, company management will have to consider changes in accounting practices in order to properly define the IT investment.

Most companies follow standard accounting practices in dealing with IT expenditures. Hardware costs are capitalized and amortized over an estimated economic life. The length of the amortization period is a compromise between physical and technical obsolescence with the current trend toward shorter life cycles. Software development and maintenance and data collection and management are treated as period expenses, and are written off when spent.

This standard accounting approach ignores the purpose for which certain IT expenditures are made. It is addressed to accountability and not to measurement. It inhibits long-term investments in technology (page D-1, October 13, 1986 *New York Times* article on "Cost Accounting's Blind Spot"). This is especially true of long-term efforts that involve software and data. Software development costs frequently exceed hardware costs, and the result can be a product that survives several generations of hardware.

A great number of programs that were written in the 1960s and 1970s are still running on IBM 308x and 309x hardware systems. Databases are being built that will serve as the data source both for systems currently in use and for systems to be built in the future. These databases will have a value and a useful life of their own, transcending any one system or application. They will be accessed by many organizations in a company and in some cases by customers and suppliers. To treat the cost of designing and building these databases as a period expense does not recognize their true purpose and value.

It is difficult for a business organization to make a large expenditure for a long-term project and then use that expenditure to measure current performance, because the investment is for software and data management. As a result some projects are not undertaken. When hardware is included in a project, a long-term view is used to justify it. The same practice should be followed for software and data.

The changes needed in accounting practice to accommodate the creation of an IT asset must take into account the different purposes of software and data-management expenditures. The items included in the asset should be:

- Expenditures made to create or purchase a software product that has an economic life and value beyond the current budget year;
- Costs of designing and building a database that will be useful beyond the current budget year;
- Costs involved with the design and construction of the telecommunications network to support data as well as voice;
- Costs of the hardware used to support the above.

These items define the IT infrastructure plus long-term development efforts. These investments should be treated as creating a capital asset and they should be amortized over the economic life of the asset. While this practice does not conform to current accounting practice, it is a recognition of a new capital good, and current accounting practice should be reexamined to deal with this new reality. Furthermore, handling long-term IT investments to include software and data collection will aid in the development of business measures of IT value.

The IT Asset for Measurement

From a measurement point of view, the benefits of creating the IT asset are as follows:

- Proper measurement of performance for IS departments engaged in Category One activities. If the IS department is using its resources to build the company's information infrastructure—an important responsibility of IS—then treating this investment as period costs of running the department is misleading. The result of the effort is a long-term capability, which the company can use to build IT applications, and the investment should be treated accordingly.

- Proper measurement of the business efforts that benefit from the existence of the IT infrastructure by taking into consideration the value of the investment and its time horizon. With an infrastructure in place, a number of IT activities (Categories One, Two, and Three) will be undertaken that make use of it. These activities will take place over the life of the asset. By amortizing the asset, a portion of the investment will be placed into the cost of the business projects during the time that they benefit from the use of the asset. The investment needs of the business projects will be properly stated over the time period that they are active.
- Proper measurement of the top management of the company. The IT infrastructure is a company asset and should be treated as such on the company's books. As the infrastructure is used to support the various company business efforts, its cost is liquidated by inclusion in the business cost structure. This properly states the business investment over time; it also shows that the company is taking advantage of the IT resource to conduct its business. For an unused asset, the amortization should be charged against the cost of managing the company and put in the management overhead. This would indicate that the asset is being underutilized.
- Proper evaluation of new technical projects, because investments for long-term efforts will be spread over time and those for infrastructure spread over a base of many projects.

IT Asset Amortization Basis

Different rules apply when determining the length of time to amortize hardware, software, and data. The period for hardware has been established and much history exists. The trend is for the period of writeoff to get shorter. This recognizes the rapid progress in improving the cost/performance of hardware. Reduced unit costs of processing power encourages upgrading and shorter writeoff periods.

The rules vary from company to company. The following is based on Financial Accounting Standards Board regulations and are typical:

Mainframes	5–7 years
Minicomputers	3–5 years
Microcomputers	2–3 years

Peripheral equipment use the same basis as the processor to which they are attached. Terminals either do the same or use 2–3 years.

Because the same history does not exist for software and data, some experience is necessary to handle non-hardware assets; experience to date is that software and data systems seem to span 2 to 3 generations of hardware. The forces contributing to this are the rapid improvements in hardware technology on the one hand, and the lack of growth in software development and data-systems technologies on the other. The amount of effort and the cost of replacing software is high enough to discourage frequent changing. The incentive is not there. As a result the software stays in place for long periods of time.

A suggested rule of thumb is this: The length of time for amortizing the non-hardware parts of the IT infrastructure is 2 to 3 times the longest life of the hardware. For a company that has mainframes in its infrastucture that are amortized over 5 years, the non-hardware parts of the infrastructure would be amortized over a period between 10 and 15 years. If software technology improves, then this time period will be reduced.

The Role of the Top IS Executive

The responsibility of the top IS executive in an enterprise is made up of some combination, possibly all, of the following:

- Planning, control, and management of an enterprise's use of information technologies in the conduct of its business.
- Development of a strategy and an infrastructure to carry out these responsibilities.
- Management of the technical staff to implement the above two points.
- Responsibility for bringing people into the organization who have the knowledge and ability to use technology and analysis in carrying out their duties. This responsibility includes the management of educational programs at all levels for both technical and managerial purposes.
- Responsibility for identifying business opportunities to use IT so that the enterprise will reap the full competitive value of the technology.
- Preparation and delivery of reports to executive management on the uses, potential uses, and business value of information technology. The latter should involve developing measurements of business value and contribution.
- Participation as a member of the executive management of the enterprise in order to identify opportunities and bring them to the attention of senior decision-makers.

The IS executive's opportunity-scanning and reporting responsibilities involve measurements of IT business value. The IS head is the company's technology executive. To get to that position, the incumbent should have a combination of business acumen and technical skills, and as a result, he or she should be a leading participant with his peers and superiors in identifying business opportunities for IT use. Therefore, to complement the other responsibilities, the IS head should have the responsibility for developing the measurements and reporting them to the company management.

Conclusion

The issue of measuring IT value is one of understanding its role and realizing its potential. Computers and communications, the main components of IT, have been available to the business world for over 30 years. In that relatively short time, the use of the technology has gone through much change and growth, with four years 1982–1986 the most dramatic. During IT's history, conflicting forces have been in play: the size of the investment, the false starts, the frequent failures to meet expectations, the lack of understanding of the technology on the part of management, and the ever-present perception of value. All of these create the need to account for and measure the contribution of IT. Although over the years many methods have been tried, most have been unsatisfactory and unsatisfying.

The purpose of this chapter has been to develop an understanding of the measurement of IT's business value. It proposes methods and measures to accomplish it. The key factor in this process is the growth of the direct use of IT for strategic and competitive purposes. A principle requirement for measuring IT business value is that IT must have a direct impact on business activities. Unless this impact exists, measurement of business value cannot be made. When IT activity supports the internal work of other organizations within an enterprise, it cannot be measured for business value.

Two important tenets of this chapter are (1) that standard business measures should be used and (2) that the business enterprise's accomplishment should be measured. Another concept is that there should be a separation between performance measurement of an organization or a department, and the measurement of the business activity of the enterprise, which consists of a number of organizations and departments.

When a company's management makes the decision to use IT for strategic and competitive purposes, then defining the measures of IT business value is included as part of the business activity. The standards for measuring are derived from management expectations and express the return looked for in pursuing the business activity.

Two other points are made in this paper. One is that the existence of an IT asset must be recognized, an asset consisting of the infrastructure made up of hardware, software, and data. The hardware has always been treated as a capital good, but the software and data have not. This is true in spite of the fact that the software and data bases often survive two to three generations of hardware. To accomplish this handling of software and data, changes have to be made in existing accounting practice.

The second point is that the head IS executive should be the one to develop the measurements and do the reporting to company management. Performing this role is consistent with the definitions of the new role for the IS head.

Finally, more research needs to be done in this area. Although we are giving attention to questions on how to use IT for competitive data on how business organizations are doing IT measurements. The data to be gathered should include the degree of IT usage as part of company business strategy; how extensively IT is used, the amount of work done in each of the three categories defined in this chapter; types of business measures used; types of measurements used for IS; types of justification used for IS projects; the role of the IS top executive; how and where IT decision-making fits into the management process; and the receptivity for changing accounting practice to accommodate the handling of an IT asset.

For most companies, IT has become an important way to conduct business. The suppliers and users of IT can be found in many of the departments and organizations that make up the company structure. A wall no longer separates the suppliers, IS, and the users of IT. The measurements of information technology have to be consistent with both business use and company organization.

Notes

1. The Diebold Group, Inc., "MIS Budgets and Key Indicators 1986," *The Diebold Research Programs Press Briefing,* unpublished, 1987.
2. Franz Edelman, "Managers, Computer Systems, and Productivity," *MIS Quarterly,* Vol. 5, No. 3, September 1981.
3. Paul A. Strassmann, "Managing the Costs of Information," *Harvard Business Review,* September–October 1976.
4. Richard L. Nolan, "Recharting DP to the Advanced Stages," *Stage by Stage,* Vol. 2, No. 3, Summer 1982.
5. Brandt Allen, "Make Information Services Pay Its Way," *Harvard Business Review,* January–February 1987.
6. Gerald L. Matlin, "What Is the Value of Investment in Information Systems?" *Published Proceedings of the Symposium on the Economics of Information Processing,* sponsored by the IBM Systems Research Institute, New York, December 15–19, 1980.
7. See note 5.
8. See note 6.
9. See note 6.
10. See note 2.
11. See note 6.
12. Michael E. Porter, *Competitive Strategy,* The Free Press, New York, 1980.
13. F. Warren McFarlan, "Information Technology Changes the Way You Compete," *Harvard Business Review,* May–June 1984.
14. Victor E. Millar, "Five Steps to Using Information for Competitive Advantage," *Journal of Information Management,* Spring 1986.
15. Charles Wiseman, *Strategy and Computers: Information Systems as Competitive Weapons,* Homewood, Illinois, Dow-Jones Irwin, 1985.
16. Gregory L. Parsons, "Information Technology: A New Competitive Weapon," *Sloan Management Review,* Fall 1983.
17. M.H. Notowidigdo, "Information Systems: Weapons to Gain Competitive Edge," *Financial Executive,* February 1984.
18. David A. Runge, *Using Telecommunications for Competitive Advantage,* Oxford University, 1985.
19. Terence A. Oliva, Diana L. Day, and Wayne S. DeSarbo, "Selecting Competitive Tactics: Try a Strategy Map," *Sloan Management Review,* Spring 1987.

IV

Measuring and Modeling the Business Value of IT

What do we measure and what measurements do we use?

Sometimes the strategic objectives on an IT project are crystal clear but the value measurements are extraordinarily complex. Such is the case, CEO John Johnson realized, with his company's moves into point-of-sale (POS) systems. The firm had implemented POS in its Midwestern retail outlets, but results from this initial implementation were decidedly mixed. Direct debit at the point of sale had cut paperwork and speeded up checkout lines at all Midwestern outlets. But after implementing POS only four stores showed any noticeable increase in sales revenue, the primary benefit the company had sought.

Johnson balked when the Vice President of Sales proposed expanding POS to all of the company's retail outlets. Johnson called on the VP to determine why POS had been successful in some stores and not in others. The company would consider expanding POS, Johnson said, but only if it could come up with a formula for "cloning" the successful POS implementations. The successful POS systems could serve as useful case studies. Any diagnostic study would have to examine many factors surrounding each local POS implementation, such as store location, size, customer demographics, and advertising budgets. The study would also have to consider

POS outputs along several dimensions, such as improved sales, reduced paperwork, and enhanced cashier productivity.

How should we evaluate and compare the performance of many similar IT implementations when inputs and outputs are numerous and complex?

In the following chapter, Robert J. Kauffman and Charles H. Kriebel present a model that cuts through the complexity of this type of microeconomic analysis. Their approach, Data Envelopment Analysis (DEA), relies on microeconomic theories of efficiency in the production process. In the context of IT, the DEA allows managers to assess the performance of systems with multiple inputs and outputs when the precise interaction among inputs and outputs is not fully understood. Kauffman and Kriebel apply their model to one such system: an automated-teller-machine (ATM) network.

Robert J. Kauffman and Charles H. Kriebel
Graduate School of Industrial Administration
Carnegie Mellon University

Dr. An Wang, the founder and chairman of Wang Laboratories, once observed that the most important technological development of the twentieth century, the computer, has been hidden in the "back room." It is hard to imagine that the computer could become more conspicuous than it is today. Information technologies (IT) permeate our society. They influence how business is conducted and determine which businesses will survive.

The performance gains of pure IT are legendary; but have the returns it contributes to enterprises exceeded the investment costs? The benefits attributed to IT range from vastly improved operating efficiencies to strategic opportunities for competitive advantage in the marketplace. Although many of these benefits are readily documented after the fact, too often the original commitment by management has relied on an act of faith. The economic climate and competitive warfare of the international economy continue to press management to reduce costs and improve efficiency. Yet in this belt-tightening period of declining budgets (for most areas), expenditures in information systems (IS) and telecommunications continue to grow at near alarming rates. Are IS budgets out of control? Is one's firm spending too much or, maybe, not enough? How can managers know, or doesn't it make any difference? In this arena today, the critical problem that confronts top management is how to determine the business value of information technologies in order to guide investment decisions.

Of course, many investments in IT are predetermined; that is, one can't be in business without the capability. (The telephone is a typical example.) However, most investment decisions have room for discretion, and hence top management needs a procedure to discriminate among alternatives. The theory for guiding this process rationally is the concept of cost/benefit analysis. To that end, a common mechanism is the calculation of net present value (NPV) or the discounting of future cash flows (DCF) associated with investment at an appropriate interest rate. The logic underlying NPV or DCF is not faulty; the procedure has been employed in industry for over 75 years. The Achilles' heel in applying this approach realistically to IT investments is the benefits component of the cash-flow equation.

More often than not, management is unable to estimate and quantify the full magnitude of benefits realizable from an investment in IT at the time the go or no-go decision is required. For example, the greatest actual benefits may result from the new business opportunities available after an IT-based infrastructure (for example, a telecommunications network or an integrated electronic office) is in place, but in the short run the IT investment adds to, rather than reduces, operating costs. These higher-order and often indirect contributions tend to be ignored in DCF analyses because they are difficult to address and understand. Given the wide range of management experience, the actual performance of IT in industry, and competitive pressures, the fallback temptation is to make at least some of the investments on faith in the future. This is hardly a satisfying resolution, although wishful thinking can be a strong deterrent for hard analysis.

This chapter discusses an approach for bridging the gap between rational-decision theory and management practice. It presents a new method of analysis and an illustrative application of the approach. The next section briefly reviews some basic concepts of performance measurement, efficiency, productivity, and economic contributions or value-added. It also examines existing management accounting practices and the complications they create in developing business-value measures of IT from conventional data sources. The following section provides an overview of a new, action-oriented method of productivity assessment, Data Envelopment Analysis (DEA). The chapter continues with a discussion of a real-world application of the technique to IT: assessing the business value of automated teller machines (ATMs) for retail payment networks in financial services. The chapter concludes with several prescriptive observations on the approach, the application, and the problem in general.

Some Basic Definitions, Concepts, and Principles

The effective analysis of performance presupposes an understanding of some basic ideas. The underlying discipline for the concept of business value is economics. Business value subsumes goal attainment, relative scarcity (or effort), and economic worth. Informed management action is the key to achieving business value in a firm.

Measurement, Efficiency, Productivity, and Economic Contribution

Measurement provides a unit of analysis. The process of measurement involves the definition and calibration of a metric, determination of a reference, standard, and goal, monitored observations, comparison of observation against the standard, and a record of the result. The critical step in this sequence is defining an appropriate measure (or several), because to a large degree the measure determines the effectiveness of the process and relative ease or difficulty in executing it. Factors that weigh in establishing measures include the criteria in Exhibit 3. While all of these factors should be recognized, the importance of any of the criteria depends on management objectives for assessing performance; consequently, application of the criteria varies with purpose.

For example, the purpose or function to be served by the measure can substantially influence which measures are relevant. The NPV or payback period may be entirely adequate for analyzing isolated equipment investments, but it is inadequate for comparing strategic opportunities from new products or services. The accuracy required will influence the available methods and feasible measures (for example, for purposes of planning,

Exhibit 3.
Criteria Influencing Definition and Choice of Performance Measures

Purpose or Function: What is the measurement goal? What is the organizational level, scale, and scope of analysis?

Accuracy Required: What is the significance of measurement errors or randomness ("noise") in the environment?

Validity or Relevance: As a performance indicator, does the measure encompass important inputs and outputs (is it monitoring the right things) and create the right incentives?

Consistency and Reliability: Does the measure yield comparable results under similar conditions (inputs)? Over time?

Responsiveness or Sensitivity: Does the measure reflect changes in the environment in a timely manner?

Quantifiability: Is the measure numerical, multi-dimensional, or formula-based?

Practicality: What is the cost of establishing the measure (time required to understand, design, and build; people effort involved; data required)?

Informativeness: Will the measure aid decision-making or problem identification?

Generality or Transferability: Can the measure and approach be used by different units of the organization?

interest is often focused on general trends or direction and not on absolute numbers). Existing data and data sources will also circumscribe the opportunities for analysis. The simple fact of the matter is that performance measurement is complex in all aspects: calculation, monitoring, evaluation, and implementation. From a pragmatic viewpoint, the important consideration is to do relative comparisons with a standard or benchmark and not with absolute figures of merit.

One baseline reference for performance is the concept of efficiency. An engineer defines efficiency (for the proverbial black box) as the ratio of (its) output to input. For comparisons over time, the engineer may define a base-period efficiency as the initial condition of a process, and then compute index numbers for future periods as the ratio of each period's efficiency relative to the base in the form of a time series. The economist's equivalent concept of efficiency is captured in the theory of production (or the theory of the firm).

Exhibit 4 is an abstract and oversimplified characterization of a production process; it depicts physical output (production) in terms of two required inputs to the process (for example, Input 1 might be labor hours and Input 2 units of a raw material). The diagram assumes that the process represents the best practice or state-of-the-art technology for the production of this output. That is, for a given level of output, the curve labeled X-X′ represents possible tradeoffs between the two inputs to produce that level of output with known production technology. Point A on the curve X-X′, for example, employs more of Input 1 to produce the given output relative to Input 2, and the opposite is true for point B on the same curve. However, both points A and B are equivalent in terms of their *technical efficiency*—each employs the same technology. This property is assumed true for all points (that is, the locus of all the combinations of the inputs, in addition to A and B) that lie on curve X-X′; and the curve is referred to as an *isoquant* or a *production frontier.* (The dashed-line curve labeled Y-Y′ is an analogous production frontier; however, it corresponds to a higher level of physical output because it lies above X-X′ in the diagram.)

Point C in Exhibit 4 lies above and to the right of the production frontier X-X′ (in the interior of the curve) and corresponds to inefficient production of the given output level, because it requires more of both inputs. A measure of the inefficiency of point C can be computed as the ratio of the line segments OA to OC relative to 100 percent. That is, the fraction OC/OA minus 1.0 multiplied by 100 percent represents the excess amount of inputs employed by production at point C above the production frontier to yield the same level of output. Movement along a production frontier such as X-X′ corresponds to substitution of one input factor for the other (which is assumed to be continuous here) and the slope of a tangent line to the curve at any given point is called the *rate of technical substitution* between the inputs. A

Exhibit 4.
A Graph of Production Economics

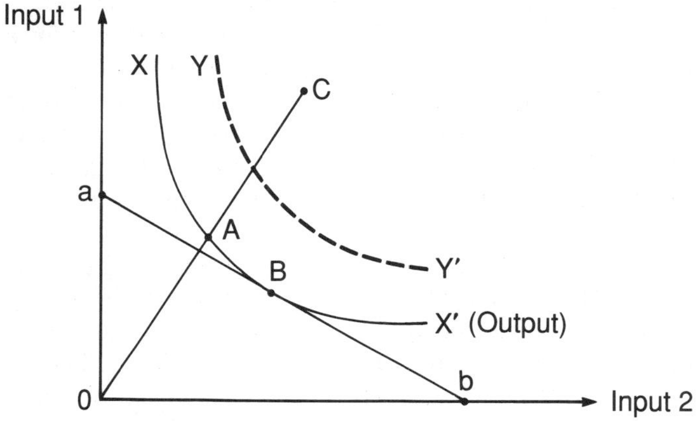

change in one input with respect to a unit change in output is referred to as the *marginal product* of that input. This concept of marginal product is closely related to that of *productivity* as discussed below.

In Exhibit 4, points A and B on the frontier are both technically efficient and hence equivalent in these terms. Is there any basis for preferring one combination of inputs over another? Economics gives the answer to this question in terms of the prices of the inputs (or their cost). That is, suppose in Exhibit 4 line a-b corresponds to the cost of the fixed inputs for the specified output, assuming the firm buys the inputs in perfectly competitive markets at constant unit prices.[1] The slope of line a-b is the negative of the input-price ratio. Then optimizing behavior (profit-maximizing or cost-minimizing) for the firm dictates that production should occur at point B, that is, at the mix of inputs on curve X-X′ that is a tangent point to the cost (input price) line a-b. This theoretical solution is optimal with respect to *economic* (or allocative) *efficiency*. As such, it equates the value of the marginal product (output price multiplied by marginal product) of each input to the input price (or unit cost), given the assumption.

To clarify, a simple numerical example of production economics is shown in Exhibit 5. The upper portion of the exhibit assumes that the X-X′ output curve in Exhibit 4 is fixed at a level of five units. The columns labeled Input 1 and Input 2 display different combinations of the inputs that will yield this same output given the technology; for example, five units of Input 1 and five units of Input 2 or two units of Input 1 and 12.5 units of Input 2, etc. The last column in Exhibit 5 shows the total cost of producing the output, assuming the per-unit prices of the inputs are $2 and $1, respectively.

From these data one sees that for an output level of five the minimum production cost is $14.13, which employs 3.5 units of Input 1 and 7.07 units of Input 2. This input combination would correspond to point B in Exhibit 4. The data in the lower portion of Exhibit 5 illustrate comparisons for a higher level of output, eight units, such as might correspond to the curve Y-Y′ in Exhibit 4. Finally, if one assumes that point A in Exhibit 4 corresponds to the inputs (7.07, 3.5), then point C with respective inputs of 10.6 and 5.25 represents an inefficiency level of 50 percent; that is, point C requires 50 percent more of each of the inputs to yield the same output level of five as the efficient point A.

The economist's perspective on technical and economic efficiency is essentially a statement about productivity and production factors (inputs and process). This differs somewhat from the conventional view in management accounting where the emphasis is on financial factors. That is, profitability analysis traditionally associates a change in profits with a change in revenues minus the change in costs (see vertical center blocks in Exhibit 6).

In a recent paper Banker, Datar, and Kaplan[2] argue that the traditional approach arises naturally in accounting where the focus of investigation is on the income statement, which segments revenues and expenses. The analysis can be extended incrementally by factoring revenues into the components of output quantity sold multiplied by unit sales price, and factoring costs into the components of quantities of inputs employed multiplied by unit input prices (see the top and bottom row sequence of blocks in Exhibit 6). As a result, changes in profits can be explained by a variance analysis of changes in each of the components added together in the profit equation. The American Productivity Center[3,4] has provided an alternative explanation

Exhibit 5.
Production Numerical Example

	Output	Input 1	Input 2	Total Cost (P_1=2, P_2=1)
X-X′:	5	25.00	1.00	$51.00
	5	7.07	3.50	17.67
	5	5.00	5.00	15.00
	5	4.00	6.25	14.25
	5	3.50	7.07	14.13
	5	3.00	8.30	14.30
	5	2.00	12.50	16.50
Y-Y′:	8	6.00	10.70	$22.70
	8	5.65	11.30	22.60
	8	5.00	12.80	22.80

Exhibit 6.
Components of Change in Profits

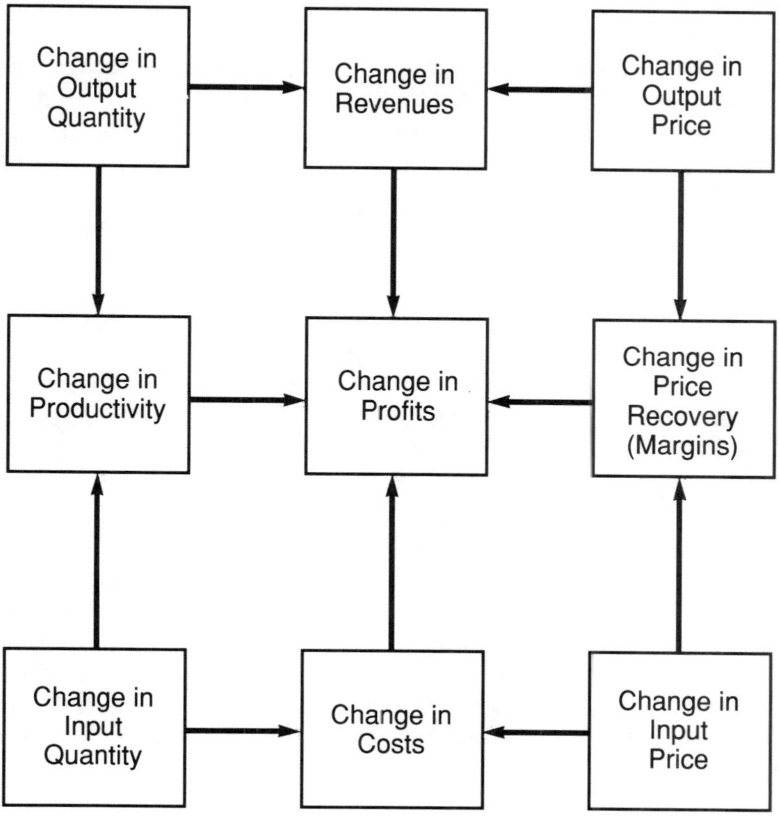

of profit variance (profitability ratio) in terms of a change (ratio) in productivity multiplied by a change (ratio) in margins or price recovery. This analysis can also be extended as before by factoring productivity into the ratio of output quantities to input quantities and factoring margins into the ratio of product-output prices to input-resource prices (see the far left and right vertical column sequences of blocks in Exhibit 6).

The cited paper by Banker, Datar, and Kaplan[5] addresses several of the problems involved with either of the aforementioned approaches to profitability analysis. One of these concerns the issue of multiple inputs and multiple outputs, and the need to relate and convert partial measures of productivity and price recovery into total factor equivalents (for example, see Craig and Harris, 1973).[6] Another concern is that performance measures in isolation (such as productivity) are not very meaningful. They acquire significance only when they are juxtaposed to comparable measures for other business units or prior time-periods to accommodate relative comparisons of performance.

The production-frontier approach can be used to analyze multiple inputs and multiple outputs with little difficulty. Even though for convenience the illustration in Exhibit 4 is limited to two inputs and one output, the mathematics of the approach has no such computational restriction. The example also suggests how measures, such as efficiency/productivity, can be calculated employing the frontier. Exploring the frontier along different input-resource dimensions can focus on key cost-drivers and potential opportunities for management action.

Profit improvement through cost management is only one aspect of the performance opportunity set. The *marginal value* (revenue) *product* defined above constitutes the gross economic contribution or gross value-added of an input resource (process) to the firm's output. (This is not the value added at the margin in terms of profits.) For some input resources, such as the conversion of a natural raw material into a finished product, the economic contribution is direct and can be readily calculated from engineering and accounting data. However, for many other resources such as IT, the contribution is more indirect. It involves one input and many outputs or many inputs and many outputs, and its primary impact (value) obtains through higher-order rather than first-order effects. In this regard IT is notorious because of its pervasiveness throughout the organization. Its contribution depends on other primary input resources, notably people; there is a time displacement between acquisition of IT capabilities and the organizational learning required to realize economic returns.

Management Accounting and the Data Problem

The American Productivity Center's (APC) approach to profit variability through productivity and price-recovery analysis employs actual quantities and prices/costs for calculating comparative ratios and change. This differs from an accountant's variance analysis using a standard-cost system that specifies input and output relationships in terms of product standards for labor, material, and overhead. Accounting standard cost systems also assume a separable and linear (constant marginal product) production technology. Banker, Datar, and Kaplan[7] discuss procedures for reconciling these differences (that is, APC measures in terms of standard costs) and they describe profit variance as the sum of sales-activity variance, productivity variance, and price-recovery variance.

While standard-cost systems and other accounting data structures can provide a wealth of information for management decisions, they do not serve the direct needs of business value measurement analysis, particularly in the context of IT. Nonetheless, it is foolhardy to ignore or discount the inertia of the existing accounting infrastructure.

As an illustration, in August 1985 the Financial Accounting Standards Board (FASB) released a recommendation (Statement 86) concerning professional practice for the treatment of the costs of IT as either a capital investment or an expense (Young, 1986).[8] The accepted practice for the costs of purchased hardware and most purchased software is to capitalize them as an investment over some useful life of service. The accounting for the cost of internally developed software is less straightforward. Common practice has been (and in all likelihood will continue to be) to expense software development costs within the accounting period; that is, to write them off in the fiscal year in which they were incurred. This asymmetric treatment of IT costs presents major difficulties for analyzing IT opportunities, especially since software accounts for more than 60 percent of the total. The treatment also runs counter to much of the conventional wisdom regarding R&D planning and investment decisions. The software development required for most major IT products typically has a useful economic half-life on the order of three to five years; but the accounting conventions, such as ROA/ROI or DCF, for IT assets tend to overemphasize the physical-capital considerations in the analysis. From the creation of the IT asset and its maintenance over a productive life (for example, through required enhancements), software costs become current expenses that may not coincide in time with their economic returns.

Business Value Measures of IT

The net economic contribution of an input resource to an output product is measured by the unit profit (sales price minus cost) of the output multiplied by the marginal product of the input. Where the input contribution to output is direct and the relative impact is focused, this statement becomes operational as an exercise in arithmetic. However, as has already been observed in the case of IT, the contribution to output is usually indirect, and different technologies have different kinds of impacts (for example, ATMs or point-of-sale (POS) terminal devices vs. telecommunications networks or an IS infrastructure). The more diffuse the impact on the firm the less direct business value can be attributed to IT. Moreover, IT business value measures should not be confused with criteria intended to track the performance of the IS organization as an entity. While the latter issue is important on its own, it is a different management consideration, which is not synonymous with IT business value.

One approach to the diversity of potential impacts from IT is through a classification of IT applications that can facilitate the identification and selection of appropriate measures by type (administrative cost reduction [ACR], productivity improvements, customer service in marketing, new product strategies, etc.) Historically the problem has been the mindset that relies on one or two direct measures, such as ACR, and attempts to employ it for all application opportunities regardless of type. This bias in IT portfolios is well known.

Business value measures should be derived from senior management goals, which in turn acquire coherence as the building blocks of the firm's corporate strategy. From the pluralism of this principle, it follows that a system of measures (not a single measure) must be employed. Despite the seductive appeal of a unitary conceptual measure, such as shareholder wealth, operationally it appears that no candidate readily decomposes into a convenient hierarchy of consistent subgoals. For example, the concept of quality must be a component of the measurement system, but its translation entails multiple dimensions, some involving subjective, or personal, judgments.

The resolution of this issue begins with top management establishing within the organization an institutional framework for measurement and monitoring. This institutional framework should target management decision and actions (for example, make or buy, capital/labor tradeoffs, and the like). It should also facilitate incorporation of a process so that the organization can determine policy, procedures, and methods for developing possible new business-value measures.[9,10]

A Management Action-Oriented Approach: Data Envelopment Analysis (DEA)

Production environments outside manufacturing place special demands on the tools managers use for productivity and performance assessment. Historical reliance on accounting, engineering, and operations as sources of data may have served manufacturing environments reasonably well, but they appear inadequate in meeting the needs of service environments where qualitative indicators may dominate results. This is especially true when managers attempt to gauge the business value of IT as an input to, or mediator of, production.

Productivity Assessment with DEA

One approach that can enhance one's ability to measure the business value of IT is Data Envelopment Analysis. DEA is a nonparametric frontier analysis approach to estimating production correspondences. It enables a manager to distinguish between efficient units lying on the frontier, and those that are less efficient and lie inside the frontier. The DEA is based on mathematical programming and production economics.

Using DEA initially requires managerial judgment in order to identify input resources that are transformed by the productive technology into a set of output commodities. Recently, DEA has been extended so that its productivity measures hold up in a variety of production environments and managerial evaluation requirements. Banker, Charnes, and Cooper,[11] for example, extended DEA to enable a manager to decompose overall inefficiency measures into resource waste and scale effects. Banker[12] provides a method to identify the most productive scale size. Other extensions involve efficiency measurement in production environments that have fixed or categorical inputs or outputs, and the identification of resource-allocation inefficiencies.

Management Action Orientation and Applications to Nontraditional Production Environments

DEA is attractive for the assessment of IT performance because of its management action orientation. Unlike other productivity assessment techniques, DEA provides measures that can lead to managerial decisions congruent with maximizing profit in nontraditional production environments. DEA does not require a prespecified functional form for the production correspondence being investigated. For example, consider how hard-pressed a manager would be to define the input-output relationship between a microcomputer on his desk and his division's sales revenue. Yet, the characterization of a frontier representing best observed performance can suggest performance targets for less efficient units and overall resource allocation involving IT.

Because IT is often an input to a multiple-input-and-output production environment, DEA is appropriate. It provides strong measures that are sensitive to the input and output mix. Productivity ratings can also be explained in terms of aspects of the managerial environment within and beyond a manager's control. This helps a decision-maker to identify and adapt to the key influences on production.

DEA has been applied to a number of IT and services settings, including the analysis of the economic impact of IT on organizations,[13] bank-branch operating efficiency,[14] corporate voice-communication-network performance,[15] and data-center efficiency.[16] It has also been combined with multivariate regression and a logit model to explain how programmer experience and the introduction of a structured analysis method affect the productivity ratings of software development teams.[17]

An Application—Retail Payment Networks in Financial Services and ATM Technology

Retail payment networks including ATMs, point-of-sale debit cards, and credit cards are among the new electronic financial services that have fundamentally changed the ways people effect cash transactions. Today more than 70,000 machines have been installed nationwide, and the number is still growing. According to one estimate, the industry spent more than $2 billion on retail electronic funds transfer between 1982 and 1985.[18] That figure is expected to balloon to at least $20 billion by the year 2000, when participants in the financial services industry will have extended retail electronic funds transfer into a communications network linking nearly 50,000 firms.[19] As retail payment networks continue to grow, their operators require improved tools to evaluate their resource consumption, cost efficiency, and effectiveness as delivery mechanisms for a variety of financial services. This section considers an application of DEA aimed at developing methods to help financial-service managers measure the business value and contribution to corporate goals provided by ATMs.

From Usage to Business Value: A New Approach to Performance Measurement

Current evaluation methods for ATMs rely heavily on rules of thumb to assess performance. For example, network managers often try to overcome the "33 percent wall," that is, convincing more than 33 percent of their ATM cardholders to perform more than three or four transactions at an ATM each month. For individual ATMs, a usage criterion may distinguish between acceptable and unacceptable performance. For supermarkets and other locations where a bank may be required to pay the host for ATM installation, the generation of an acceptable level of interchange fees may be most important. (Interchange fees are fees charged by a bank when other banks' customers use its ATMs.)

These performance measures provide an incomplete picture of the business value that an ATM network can provide to a bank. Surpassing the "33 percent wall" for active ATM card use may only be important if the convenience of card use can be linked to customer willingness to leave deposits with the bank. Other times, it may be important to promote cost control in bank branches.

Card usage is not the best surrogate for business value in other situations. For example, usage will not provide a good surrogate for business value when transaction levels are similar. Instead, one should value an ATM more highly if it serves a clientele leaving a higher level of deposits. However, to do so one must first test whether ATMs, and the convenience they provide, influence customers to leave deposits with the bank.

Another example in which usage is misleading involves the impact ATMs have on branch costs. For similar usage levels, ATMs at branches with expensive teller labor save a bank more money.

Current rules of thumb are also unreliable because they do not address the context dependency of production at an ATM. For example, competitive pressures for deposits among banks, the density of network ATMs in a region, and the presence of a competing ATM network are all likely to affect an ATM's business value. The following sections demonstrate that it is possible to build more consistent and robust measures for the business value of ATMs.

The Production Process for ATM Services

The creation of ATM services is a microeconomic production process. Gauging the productivity of such a process involves quantifying input resources, and capturing the process by which inputs are transformed into service and other outputs that represent benefits derived by the bank. Production occurs at an individual ATM under the influence of market and other conditions called *exogenous factors*. Exogenous factors are those over which management has little short-run control. Some examples are local demographics, participation in a shared ATM network of regional or national scope, and coverage by competitors' ATMs. Each of these factors can condition a manager's expectations for an ATM's business value.

Location strategy factors also influence production at an ATM. They describe the bank's business goals that drive the location of an ATM. One example of a location strategy is locating an ATM where other banks' customers are likely to use it to earn interchange fees. Network management can exercise discretion in the location, configuration, and service quality associated with each ATM. But the actual performance of an ATM is likely to be significantly influenced by the strategic choice underlying its location. Thus, location strategy factors are *endogenous* influences in our model. A representation of the ATM production process is shown in Exhibit 7.

Direct and Indirect ATM Outputs: The Business Value Linkage

A basic characteristic of the production process for an individual ATM is that it yields direct and indirect outputs. Direct ATM outputs are those that can be measured directly at the ATM. An obvious example is the number of transactions involving cash withdrawals, deposits, or transfers. Direct ATM outputs are local outputs of the production process. Knowing their

Exhibit 7.
The Production Process for ATM Services

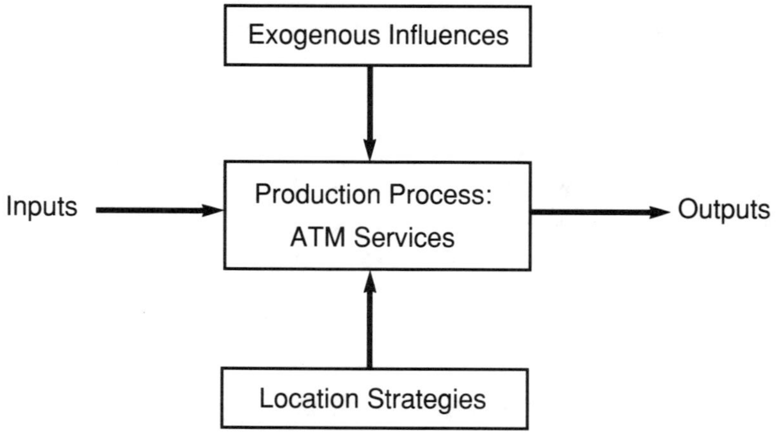

quantity, however, provides little information about the economic contribution of an ATM to the bank in the absence of information about its operating context.

Indirect ATM outputs are those that cannot be measured directly at the ATM level; they are tangible at higher levels of the firm. An example is the contribution an ATM transaction makes to reducing direct teller-labor hours for retail transaction processing at a nearby bank branch. Such indirect outputs are nonlocal outputs for an individual ATM, because their impacts are felt at the branch or bank levels. Nevertheless, in order to carry out an evaluation of an ATM's economic performance, one requires a means of determining their values at the local ATM level. Specifically, in the context of Exhibit 3, one needs to answer questions such as:

1. At what organizational levels do the indirect outputs of individual ATMs become measurable?
2. What are the underlying production processes associated with the relevant organizational levels?
3. How can one use the knowledge of these production processes to attribute business value from the indirect outputs to individual ATMs?

One identifies the business-value linkage between direct and indirect ATM outputs by considering more aggregated levels of production within the organization. For example, the contribution of an ATM to the reduction of bank labor primarily makes an impact on the production processes associated with nearby branches. The ATMs displace human labor to the extent that they handle transactions that would have been handled at a teller's window of a branch. Thus, one needs to identify those ATMs that can contribute to the production process of a particular branch.

To do this, we define the branch operating territory as the local region around the branch that the bank perceives to be its primary service area. Operationally, this region is defined in terms of U.S. population census tracts. By identifying the nearby tracts where people who have accounts at the branch live, we establish the branch operating territory where the majority of account holders tend to cluster. Branch operating territories can otherwise be defined consistent with the bank's internal operating policies. Not all branches need to have the same size territories, and the territories need not be entirely disjoint. In any case, ATMs and competitive branches located in this region are identified as members of the branch operating territory.

Exhibit 8 shows a sample aggregation for two branch operating territories of Bank A. Bank A competes with three other banks: B, C, and X. Banks A, B, and C operate a number of ATMs on the same shared ATM network. Bank X operates two ATMs on a competing network. To illustrate the relationships among the competitors, focus on Branch Operating Territory A20. In this territory, Bank A's branch competes for deposits with Bank C's branch. A and C also operate ATMs in the territory, A3 and C1 respectively. In the same territory Bank X operates ATM X2, which cannot be shared by customers of A, B, and C. In this territory, only A3 and C1 can contribute to Branch A20's production process; X2 cannot contribute.

Development of a retail deposit base in a region involves competition among banks, which configure branch and ATM networks through which a variety of financial services is delivered. This configuration is called the retail service cluster. In the example above, Bank A has a retail service cluster that consists of branch operating territories A10 and A20. The bank's service-delivery configuration, relative to those of its competitors, determines its ability to gather a retail deposit base. This cluster concept is quite flexible. Clusters can be built up in terms of a bank's own view of its regional retail markets. The county level, for example, is one basis to define a cluster of branches and ATMs, though a higher or lower level of aggregation might be used.

Business value is attributed to an ATM using multivariate regression to identify the significance of the presence of ATMs among other factors in the production of retail deposits. This approach is in the mainstream of literature on bank-branch performance (for example, Hansen and Weinberg[20] and Olsen and Lord[21]). Yet it has not been possible to identify any studies that include variables to describe the impact that retail-payment technologies might have on branch performance. A representative regression involves

Exhibit 8.
Branch Operating Territory and Retail Service Cluster Aggregations

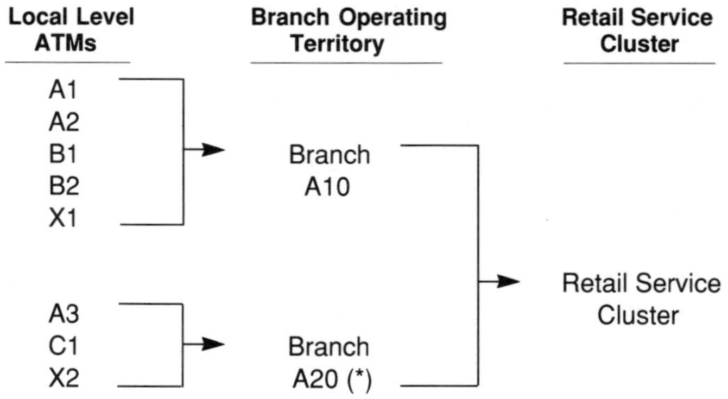

Key
A signifies an ATM or branch belonging to Bank A
B signifies an ATM belonging to Bank B, A's competitor on *same network*
C signifies an ATM belonging to Bank C, A's competitor on *same network*
X signifies an ATM belonging to Bank X, A's competitor on *another network*
*signifies that Branch #A20 competes with a branch owned by Bank C nearby

estimating the amount of deposits captured by a branch as a function of various branch operating territory variables. These variables include:

- Territory Demographics: Census tract descriptors, including population, average income, etc.
- Branch Characteristics: Variables that describe branch service facilities, such as
  - number of teller and platform stations
  - presence of bank-run ATMs
  - presence of walk-up and drive-up facilities
  - time in place
  - dummy variables for variety of service levels the branch provides
  - interest rate on deposit products
  - recognition of bank's name in the consumer marketplace
- Competitor Branches: Number of competitors' branches in territory
- Shared ATMs: Number of shared ATMs in territory
- Competitors' ATMS: Number of nonshared ATMs in territory

Assuming this simple explanatory model has been validated and the ATM variables are significant, then the regression yields a coefficient for the presence of bank-operated ATMs in the set of branch-design variables. It also gives coefficients of contribution for other shared ATMs, and the negative impact of nonshared ATMs on other retail payment networks.

Alternate models involve estimations of demand and savings deposits separately, or even the number of these accounts that a branch is able to gain, provided information on the competition is publicly available. Multiplying the regression coefficient for an ATM by the amount of deposits at a branch gives a simple measure of ATM contribution. If the ATM variables are not significant in this regression, then there are grounds for arguing that ATMs are not providing business value by protecting a deposit base. Subsequent analysis of ATM performance should exclude this output variable.

A similar multivariate regression approach is used to identify average teller processing times, specific to different branch environments, for transactions that could be handled by an ATM. Then, using data for the direct transaction and uptime outputs from bank-operated ATMs in the branch operating territory, one can calculate an implied value for the hours of teller labor contributed by the ATM.

DEA Assessment

Although the authors have proposed a method to attribute business value to ATMs, one still needs to consider whether that value has been efficiently produced. To perform this assessment, Data Envelopment Analysis is applied to a sample 30-ATM network. The inputs and outputs of the ATMs in this network are shown in Exhibit 9. One assumes that the bank will have initially performed the ATM business-value estimations described earlier. The analysis also requires operating data on the number of interchange revenue-generating transactions, the support trips made to maintain an ATM in a period, and the average working capital on hand at a machine. The latter two represent the primary variable costs for ATM locations. Utilizing an appropriate DEA formulation,[22] the authors arrived at the sample results shown in the far right column of Exhibit 9.

The DEA results measure the technical efficiency of ATM production. The focus is on input resource waste. All ATMs that rated 1.000 occupy positions on the production frontier. They consume the least input resources, given their output levels. Those that rate less than 1.000 are technically inefficient. Seven ATMs have efficiency ratings of less than 0.800: A3, A4, A17, A18, A23, A24, and A25. These represent roughly the bottom quartile in efficiency. Management should more carefully study the circumstances of their production and performance to determine whether working capital and maintenance trips can be reduced while output levels are maintained.

Exhibit 9.
Data Set and Results for a Sample ATM Network

	OUTPUTS			INPUTS		
ATM	Interchange Transactions (1000s)	Deposit Contribution ($1000s)	Labor Contribution (Hours)	Working Capital ($1000s)	Maintenance Trips	Technical Efficiency Rating
A1	2.0	300	150	15	12	1.000
A2	2.4	272	122	36	5	.862
A3	1.0	250	150	25	12	.785
A4	1.0	250	100	25	10	.583
A5	1.0	200	50	25	5	.858
A6	1.0	200	100	15	5	1.000
A7	2.0	150	150	15	8	.961
A8	2.0	150	100	15	8	.939
A9	3.0	100	200	15	10	1.000
A10	3.0	100	250	15	12	1.000
A11	2.5	300	200	30	6	1.000
A12	2.5	275	125	35	4	1.000
A13	2.4	273	125	37	5	.857
A14	2.6	225	215	24	7	1.000
A15	2.6	215	190	24	7	.944
A16	2.6	230	180	18	9	1.000
A17	2.7	125	160	23	11	.708
A18	2.7	125	162	25	12	.717
A19	2.9	130	75	19	4	1.000
A20	2.6	216	192	26	9	.820
A21	1.1	80	95	17	5	.952
A22	0.5	50	125	22	6	.869
A23	0.6	125	110	18	8	.778
A24	0.9	70	80	20	8	.700
A25	1.4	90	60	20	6	.780
A26	1.9	250	85	14	5	1.000
A27	0.6	225	115	16	9	.887
A28	0.8	220	120	17	10	.837
A29	0.9	160	130	15	11	.933
A30	1.2	110	155	14	8	1.000

Exhibit 10 presents additional results from DEA for the lowest quartile to guide managerial action further. The rating for ATM A3 of 0.785, for example, is based on a comparison to a weighted average of the efficient ATMs in its reference set: A1, A11, A14, and A26. This composite ATM lies on the multifaceted production frontier. It can be thought of as a target for the inefficient ATM's improvement. Notice also that A17 and A18 have identical referent sets. This implies that these ATMs possess relatively similar, though not identical, input and output mixes. Management should probe how to improve the performance of A17 and A18 by investigating why A9, A14, A19 , and A26, which have similar input-output mixes, are on the nearby frontier. This kind of analysis allows managers to design policies to improve operating efficiency, policies that reflect the circumstances of production.

A word of caution in the use of these results is in order. It is important for managers to understand how the exogenous environment affects the creation of ATM-related outputs. It is unlikely that, in the absence of changes in the exogenous environment, changes to the input variables can lead to substantial changes in the business value of outputs. Thus, the analysis proposed is best suited to input reduction, where possible, and not output augmentation.

Approaching ATM performance assessment in the two-step process described above, managers may learn that the number of transactions processed at an ATM is insufficient to determine its business value. Managers should also recognize that a technically inefficient ATM can still be a good location in terms of business value. For example, ATM A4, with a rating of 0.583, is particularly inefficient. However, it is among the top 10 ATMs in terms of deposit contribution. To sharpen management's insight, one needs to determine whether production is economically efficient, that is, whether ATM-service production maximizes profit. Because a manager can

Exhibit 10.
Additional Results for a Sample ATM Network: Lowest Quartile

ATM	Rating	Reference Set
A3	.785	A1, A11, A14, A26
A4	.583	A1, A14, A16, A26
A17	.708	A9, A14, A19, A26
A18	.717	A9, A14, A19, A26
A23	.778	A26, A30
A24	.700	A26, A30
A25	.780	A19, A26

readily associate prices with each of the inputs and outputs submitted to DEA, the analysis can be extended to determine ATM profitability. This further helps management to identify ATMs that might be targets for closing.

Prescriptive Conclusions

As noted at this chapter's outset, management has a dilemma. IS budgets appear to be growing out of control and senior executives worry that their firm is spending too much on unjustified promises. But simultaneously, they are under constant economic pressure from competitive threats to exploit IT innovations for business and strategic opportunity without regard to cost.

A new approach, DEA, shows comparative competitive measures of performance can be made. Such measures based on DEA can encompass shared costs and infrastructure, and with analysis, can generate benchmarks for IT cost control.

This approach is useful for gaining an understanding of the complexity involved, but DEA is not a surgeon's hammer for IT assessment. It cannot identify all the outputs in some cases; for example, what is the value of a database management system or of electronic mail? The results from DEA are only as good as the data submitted by management for analysis.

Senior management is a necessary and vital participant in the assessment process and its role and contribution have been reasonably well-defined.[23] Top management should emphasize the portfolio aspect of IT impacts versus the evaluation of individual projects by defining multiple inputs and outputs. The DEA analysis can capture the interrelationship involved, but to be effective it requires management ingenuity and insight when the analysis is set up. This means defining goals, inputs, and outputs.

The general problem every manager faces is defining the business-value linkage for IT. As argued above, both diffuse and focused impacts are possible and likely, but the impact will vary by type of IT. Moreover, not all outputs can be readily priced; for example, which prices should be assigned to outputs such as quality in an ATM context or information accuracy in a customer file. Information technologies with diffuse impacts will be the toughest to assess. For ATMs, as the foregoing example illustrated, the business-value linkage is comparatively direct. The ATM is an IT with relatively focused impacts. The long-term goal of this research and its application is to expand the range of information technologies that can be assessed well.

Subject to the preceding conditions, the computational procedures for DEA are reasonably straightforward. That is, once a model is set up, computer programs exist for computing frontiers and performing sensitivity analysis. In executing DEA the approach can facilitate learning about consequences and formulation of policy with respect to IT. But most important, this approach shifts management's focus from IT per se to business processes, linkages, contributions, value, and organizational impacts.

Overall, the approach proposed here suggests an action agenda. Senior management must first establish an institutional framework for measurement and monitoring, and further identify the core business drivers. In the process they must recognize the need for multiple measures of comparison when dealing with diffuse concepts such as quality, which requires a system hierarchy of subgoals.

The operating line managers must then identify the key transactions for the core businesses, and define the linkages and contributions of information technology to those transactions. That is, what is the added economic value from information technologies to the transactions that drive the core business areas of the firm?

Finally, analysis as characterized figuratively in the following equation should be the focus of this approach.

"MEASURE + ANALYSIS = ACTION"

The authors acknowledge the general support of the International Center for Information Technologies and Joseph Pendleton III, Senior Vice President of Electronic Banking at Meridian Bancorp, Reading, Pennsylvania, for providing financial support, access to personnel, and assistance in understanding the key issues in the management of an ATM network. The data that we present in this paper, however, have no relationship to Meridian's ATM network.

Notes

1. This diagram and analysis assumes that the total cost of production is a linear function of the inputs; for example, for input prices p1 and p2, respectively, cost = $p_1I_1 + p_2I_2 + A$ with A a constant.
2. Rajiv D. Banker, Srikant M. Datar, and Robert S. Kaplan, "Productivity Measurement and Management Accounting," working paper, Carnegie Mellon University, 1986.
3. American Productivity Center, *Total Performance Measurement*, Houston, 1981.
4. Baizil J. von Loggerenberg and Stephen J. Cucchiano, "Productivity Measurement and the Bottom Line," *National Productivity Review*, Vol. 1, Winter 1981–82.
5. See note 2.
6. C.H. Craig and R.C. Harris, "Total Productivity Management at the Firm Level," *Sloan Management Review*, Spring 1973, pp. 13–28.
7. See note 2.
8. Arthur Young, "Software Costs: Implementing the New Accounting Standard," Arthur Young International, 1986.
9. One such framework with emphasis on organization and process (not necessarily "business-value measures," per se) is Russell L. Ackoff, *A Concept of Corporate Planning*, Wiley-Interscience, 1970, especially Chapters 5 and 7. The following discussion deals more with approach and method.
10. See note 9.
11. Rajiv D. Banker, A. Charnes, and W.W. Cooper, "Models for Estimation of Technical and Scale Inefficiencies in Data Envelopment Analysis," *Management Science*, Vol. 30, 1984, pp. 1078–1092.
12. Rajiv D. Banker, "Estimating Most Productive Scale Size Using Data Envelopment Analysis," *European Journal of Operational Research*, September, 1984, pp. 35–44.
13. William C. Chismar and Charles H. Kriebel, "A Method for Assessing the the Economic Impact of Information Systems Technology on Organizations," *Proceedings of the Sixth International Conference on Information Systems*, Indianapolis, December 1986.
14. H.D. Sherman and F. Gold, "Bank Branch Operating Efficiency," *Journal of Banking and Finance*, Vol. 9, 1985, pp. 297–315.
15. R.E. Crow, "On the Efficiency of Corporate Voice Communications Networks," working paper, Dept. of Engineering and Public Policy, Carnegie Mellon University, 1987.
16. J. Elam, J. Henderson, and J. Thomas, "Evaluating the Efficiency of the Information Systems Function," working paper, University of Texas, Austin, 1985.
17. Chris F. Kemerer, "Measurement of Software Development Productivity," unpublished doctoral thesis, G.S.I.A., Carnegie Mellon University, 1987.
18. G.M. Wagner, "Increasing ATM Usage: A Strategic Perspective," *The Magazine of Bank Administration*, December 1985, pp. 18–26.
19. P.K. Coats, "Electronic Funds Transfer Networks: Modeling Their Impact on Bank Service Goals," *Computers and Operations Research*, Vol. 11, 1984, pp. 415–426.
20. M.H. Hansen and C.B. Weinberg, "Retail Market Sharing In a Competitive Environment," *Journal of Retailing*, Vol. 55, Spring 1979, pp. 37–46.

21. L.M. Olsen and J.D. Lord, "Market Area Characteristics and Branch Bank Performance," *Journal of Bank Research*, Vol. 10, 1979, pp. 102–110.
22. Rajiv D. Banker, "Productivity Measurement and Management Control," in P. Kleindorfer (Ed.), *The Management of Productivity and Technology in Manufacturing*, Plenum Publishing, New York, 1985.
23. Charles H. Kriebel, "Understanding the Strategic Investment in Information Technology," working paper, G.S.I.A., Carnegie Mellon University, 1986.

V

Business Value as Justificatory Argument

What do we measure and what measurements do we use?

Before he became CEO, John Johnson had long management experience; it had taught him the value of making a strong business case. A business case is a structured argument advancing a particular course of action. Typically, managers use quantitative value measurements such as revenue projections and cost/benefit studies to validate their case for an investment, project, or program. The case provides the context in which performance measures and targets are interpreted and applied.

Johnson thought that developing a framework for initiating, presenting, and reviewing IT business cases with an emphasis on quality argumentation would facilitate measurement of IT value. He put a premium on logical, well-thought-out, well-organized, and validated proposals. He recognized that if the firm had a methodology for assessing the soundness of IT business cases, better decisions would be made.

The Vice President of IS brought an "idea processing" microcomputer software package to Johnson's attention. This package, she claimed, could help managers prepare, review, and evaluate complex business proposals. Johnson tried the package and found it to his liking. It helped him strengthen the logical consistency of his business arguments, and diagnose faults in others' reasoning. He recommended the package to other top executives, and it soon became a corporate standard. The quality of proposals within the firm improved noticeably, because the package tied IT activities more explicitly to the business plan and gave clear measures for assessing IT performance.

How can we measure the strength of the business case for an IT investment, project, program, or policy?

In the following chapter, E. Burton Swanson outlines the elements of a solid and persuasive business case for IT investments. Swanson proposes measuring the value of a potential investment in terms of the quality of the business case—that is, the logic and the numbers—that supports it. He describes a variety of commercial idea-processing packages designed to help managers develop business cases.

E. Burton Swanson
Anderson Graduate School of Management
University of California, Los Angeles

One of the central themes in this book is that measuring the business value of information technologies is more a management problem than a technical problem. The issue presents itself in a familiar management form: the investment proposal submitted for organizational approval. The investment proposal uses management arguments to advance a possible course of action. The originators of such proposals often include measures of projected revenues and costs, or documented benefits from existing systems, as ammunition in support of their arguments. The following fictional case is intended to illustrate how measurement fits into the management process surrounding proposal inception, presentation, and review.

The XYZ Bank is among the largest in Canada.[1] In early 1986, its Retail Banking Unit is faced with organizational evaluation of its point-of-sale (POS) authorization terminal program. Begun in 1984, the program involves in part the placement of about 9,000 terminals with retail merchants by the end of 1986, at which time the cumulative capital investment will total more than $3.8 million, with additional implementation costs of $1.1 million. An operating deficit of $102,000 is projected for 1986, but, it is claimed, a full payback of investments will occur by 1988.

Point of authorization (POA) is defined as a strategic issue for the bank. Improved productivity and the reduction of operating costs are the immediate goals, to be achieved by reducing the manual interface with merchants on the one hand, and reducing fraud and credit write-off losses on the other. The desire to cement existing merchant relationships and to protect and enhance retail market share also motivate the program.

In defense of its POA program, Retail Banking has prepared a position paper. Major sections of the paper are:

- Executive Summary
- Retail Industry and its Electronic Funds Transfer at the Point of Sale (EFTPOS) Potential
- Development of EFT in the Bank

- Marketing Strategy
- Competition in POA
- Current Position in POA
- POA Communications as a Key to Profitability
- POA Benefits, Costs, and Statistics
- Resources Required
- Conclusions and Issues

Substantial uncertainties surround the POA program, making comprehensive evaluation problematic. At one level, the level at which the program was first quantitatively justified, Retail Banking claimed improved cost-effectiveness. But at another level, the strategic position of the bank in its markets is apparently the urgent issue. "Unless we lead," reads one section of the report, "we will be scrambling to counter the initiatives of other banks, near-banks, card issuers, and third-party suppliers. If we wait until all the logistic, costing, and pricing problems have been resolved before we move, the market will be gone."

How can the bank compute the bottom line of its POA program? That is, what is the business value of the program, and does this value warrant the investment? This is the measurement challenge facing bank management. It is a challenge with which many executives are familiar, in one form or another.

The central thesis of this chapter is that any purported bottom-line number embodies a management argument. Whether any measure of business value is good or not is a matter of the soundness of this underlying argument. Furthermore, the "ideal" bottom-line number is in general a measure of the strength (soundness) of the management argument. The development, analysis, and presentation of a management argument, such as that reflected in the bank's position paper, is therefore fundamental to management-decision support.

The following sections present the concept of justificatory argument as a foundation for the measurement of business value. The chapter also reviews idea-processing technology as a means for management argumentation. It uses a commercial idea-processor to explore and illustrate the justification of the XYZ Bank's POA Program. The discussion closes with a summary of the management implications of this research.

Measurement and Justificatory Argument

Measurement is commonly defined as the assignment of numbers to objects according to established rules. Thus, measurement is fundamentally quantitative. In seeking to measure the business value of information technologies, for example, one looks for appropriate rules that will "put a number on it," but such measurement rules for management are not easily identified. And the numbers placed on business value are often controversial.[2]

Reflecting such difficulties, the subject of measurement is frequently entangled in two mystiques. The first of these is the Mystique of Quantity, which the philosopher Abraham Kaplan has characterized as "an exaggerated regard for the significance of measurement, just because it is quantitative, without regard to what has been measured or to what can subsequently be done with the numbers. Number is treated as having an intrinsic scientific value."[3] The second is the Mystique of Quality, which, according to Kaplan, "also subscribes to the magic of numbers, only, it views their occult powers as a kind of black magic, effective only for evil ends, and seducing us into giving up our souls for what, after all, is nothing but dross."[4]

Quantities and qualities are not really antithetical, however. They are, in fact, complementary. Quantities are established necessarily on qualitative foundations. For example, a sound measure of business value presupposes some theory of business value.[5] Similarly, qualities are often substantiated in quantitative terms; putting a number on business value enables us to talk with authority about increases or decreases in such value.

From the point of view of supporting a decision, four types of useful measures can be identified: *suggestive* measures, which make minimal assumptions about relevance and are merely evocative of their implications; *predictive* measures, which pose alternatives for the decision-maker; *decisive* measures, which imply choice on the basis of a unifying value scale; and *systemic* measures, which place a decision in the larger context.[6] Exhibit 11 illustrates these measurements as they apply to the bank's position paper we are considering.

The decisive measure is the type most often preferred by managers. This is understandable, for it is the measure that justifies the hard choice a manager inevitably confronts. But decisive measures do not come easily; they require a unifying value scale. And because values are not easily unified by means of a metric, hard choices often remain just that.

Exhibit 11 shows that measures are also typically embedded in textual assertions. Such measurement-based assertions are the everyday stuff of management discourse. Their potency is in the arguments that surround a proposal to invest in information technology or any other capital good.

What, in general, is the nature of such an argument? According to the philosopher Steven Toulmin,

> A man who makes an assertion puts forward a claim—a claim on our attention and to our belief. . . . The claim implicit in an assertion is like a claim to a right or to a title. As with a claim to a right, though

Exhibit 11.
Types of Measurement in Decision Support

Type of Measurement	Related Excerpt from Bank Position Paper
1. Suggestive	"Current cost per voice authorization is $1.17 in the Western Region, $0.68 in the Eastern Region, and $0.51 in the Central Region."
2. Predictive	"If we could prevent a merchant from making two authorization calls a day it would reduce the Bank's costs by $26–$61 per month."
3. Decisive	"Eliminating voice authorization can cost justify a POA terminal. The total cost per month of providing a merchant with a terminal is estimated to be less than $64."
4. Systemic	"Emphasis has been placed upon reducing fraud and credit losses, which cost the bank $17.3 million in 1985; however, more money may be saved by eliminating voice authorizations, which cost $4.9 million in 1985."

> it may in the event be conceded without argument, its merits depend on the merits of the argument which could be produced in its support. Whatever the nature of the particular assertion may be . . . in each case we can challenge the assertion, and demand to have our attention drawn to the grounds (backing, data, facts, evidence, consideration, features) on which the merits of the assertion are to depend. We can, that is, demand an argument . . .[7]

Thus understood, the basic function of argument in support of an assertion is to justify that assertion.

The problem of assessing the business value of an investment in information technology is thus recast. Any such investment is advanced in an organization by the assertion that it is warranted. The justification for this claim—which extends not only to readers' and listeners' attention and belief, but also to scarce organizational resources—is a supporting argument. This is always the case, whatever the various measures used. Therefore, if there is one bottom-line number that may properly be put on any such proposed investment, it would be a measure of the strength of the justificatory argument.

How then are justificatory arguments to be assessed? If one takes them at face value, one takes them as they appear in their usual guises (for example, in formal written documents such as the position paper prepared by the Retail Banking Unit for the XYZ Bank.) One would thus read, linearly from beginning to end, the text of a document presenting an argument or else skip among the hierarchically arranged subsections in pursuit of specific issues of interest. In the end, readers ask themselves whether they have been persuaded.

But what constitutes a good argument, the kind of argument that persuades? Are the surface features of an argument as presented in a document the only features to which one should attend? Might it not be possible instead to examine arguments more systematically, in terms of the underlying structure of their ideas? These are questions addressed in the following sections.

New Technology for Argumentation

While it might be problematic to measure the strength of an IT investment proposal, advances in the technology itself provide new opportunities for effective argumentation. These advances are generally grouped under the label of *idea processing*. The concept of idea processing has gained much of its currency in association with certain commercially available microcomputer-based software products known as *outliners*. These products provide general purpose outlining in support of word processing and manuscript preparation. ThinkTank is perhaps the most well-known of these outlining tools. Framework, an integrated package, provides comparable capabilities. More recent products built around the outlining concept include MaxThink, Freestyle, and Fact Cruncher.[8]

While such outliners have much to recommend them, they are only the predecessors of more powerful tools to come. These new tools will merge "hypertext" systems with argumentation protocols in collaborative work contexts.[9] Hypertext organizes text much as databases organize data; it may be understood as a network of textual nodes joined by referential links. Where these nodes and links are also typed by means of a conceptual and logical schema, analysis of an argument embodied in hypertext may be specifically structured and thereby facilitated, as shall be illustrated shortly. Several experimental systems under development provide a glimpse of what the future promises.

One hypertext system, NoteCards, is under development at Xerox's Palo Alto Research Center (PARC). NoteCards is aimed at supporting individual knowledge workers "engaged in analyzing information, constructing models, formulating arguments, designing artifacts, and generally processing ideas."[10] At its core is an electronic generalization of the 3×5 paper notecard. Typed links provide logical connections among notes. Students have been among the early users; the thesis of one was constructed in terms of a four-level argument tree involving 20 issues, each with 3 to 7 competing hypotheses, together with supporting and rebuttal arguments and facts. NoteCards is implemented within a Xerox LISP programming environment.

Another hypertext experiment is MIKROPLIS, a microcomputer-based textbank management system developed by McCall and associates at the Gesellschaft fuer Information und Dokumentation in the Federal Republic of Germany.[11] Like NoteCards, MIKROPLIS was conceived to support professionals in collecting textual information, organizing ideas, and structuring problems. Elements of text are organized as a quasi-hierarchy. Among the first exploratory applications are: (1) idea and problem processing for technology assessment involving acid rain; (2) information storage and retrieval in support of technical glossary and thesaurus development; and (3) the explication of critical expert opinion in several fields (in support of litigation, for example).

Kandt describes a software tool he developed specifically to facilitate competitive argumentation in support of analytic knowledge work such as policy analysis.[12] The tool is motivated by his observation that "many [analytic] reports do not distinguish between evidence and conjecture, seldom indicate the completeness of coverage, rarely assess the evidence for alternative conjectures, and usually do not identify underlying assumptions."

In Kandt's tool, system knowledge is represented in terms of entities, relations, and types, and the tool uses the AP5 representation language. Permissible relations include facts, events, definitions, assumptions, and hypotheses. Knowledge "demons," statements about what can be derived from known evidence, are used to examine an argument's validity. The tool is presently implemented on several personal LISP machines.

NoteCards, MIKROPLIS, and Kandt's tool illustrate the diversity of current efforts to support argumentation. Interestingly, all are based on support of the individual knowledge worker, where the fundamental interaction is between a single person and the microcomputer-based tool. To extend this single interaction to collaboration among colleagues presumes an asynchronous process in which work is passed from one individual to another. In contrast, other current research is based on argumentation which is substantially face-to-face, and hence synchronous.

Nunamaker and colleagues at the University of Arizona have developed PLEXSYS, which "provides an integrated workbench of planning and decision models that can be used by organization planners to assist in the unstructured process of organization planning."[13] This system is made available to user groups in an MIS Planning and Decision Laboratory. Members of the group sit at networked microcomputers around a U-shaped table; a large-screen projection system supports the sharing of individual and aggregated work. The PLEXSYS knowledge base is defined in PLEXL, a process description language based on PSL/PSA. The principal application is electronic brainstorming; strategic-assumption surfacing and analyis is another.[14] To date, more than 200 planners in groups drawn from academia, government, and industry have used the system.[15]

Colab is an experimental meeting room under development at Xerox PARC. This development was motivated by the observation that "most of us use computer tools (such as word processors and spreadsheets) to help us with our work, but when we want to work as a group, we leave our computers behind."[16] This system is designed for groups of two to six professionals and is arranged similarly to the University of Arizona's MIS Planning and Decision Laboratory. Among Colab tools are Cognoter, an idea processor similar to those described above, and Argnoter, an argumentation spreadsheet based on the idea that "just as a numerical spreadsheet program provides a way of exploring entailments of hypothetical numerical relationships, an argumentation spreadsheet. . .provides a way of exploring belief entailments."[17]

Recent commercial software products such as Coordinator and For Comment further exploit the collaborative work concept, where members of a group are not assumed to be physically present in the same room.[18] However, these products assume asynchronous communication among members, and offer no explicit support of argumentation.

I conclude that convergence of idea-processing tools in support of synchronous and asynchronous collaborative work will ultimately occur, and in this context structured argumentation may play an increasingly important role.

The next section explores and illustrates the concept of structured argumentation by applying a commercial idea-processor to the analysis of the bank position paper described above.

Diagnosing a Faulty Argument

Among the most recent commercial idea-processors is Houdini, a software product of MaxThink, Inc.[19] Houdini is a hypertext-based system which supports the construction and use of a general network of ideas. Within the network, each idea at a node is associated with another by a directed link according to their relationship. Nodes, but not links, may be typed (classified and grouped). Because the system provides an accessible means for the construction of a general network of ideas and is not, like most available systems, limited to hierarchical structures, Houdini is well-suited to this chapter's exploratory and diagnostic purposes.[20] The argument to be dissected and diagnosed is the one presented in the XYZ Bank position paper described above.

Before proceeding, it is important to emphasize that this application is essentially naive, in that I am expert in neither the software nor the position paper. This, however, should not detract from the present purposes.

Houdini is a general-purpose idea processor; it imposes no conceptual or logical structure upon its hypertext network. For the present purposes, it was useful to develop and employ a specific architecture for argumentation. In doing so, I necessarily worked within the Houdini constraint that nodes, but not links, could be typed; and I attempted to minimize the complexity of the architecture, as described next.

For the purposes of this study, an argument is formally composed of three constituent parts: (1) *facts*, employed to draw (2) *conclusions*, the validity of which depends upon (3) *assumptions*. The unit of analysis within the argument is the *conclusion*.[21] Thus, a specific structure is imposed upon the argument.

Each conclusion in an argument network is understood to have its inputs and outputs. Facts constitute the basic inputs; assumptions the outputs. At least one fact and one assumption are assumed necessary for any one well-reasoned conclusion. That a conclusion should precede its assumptions in a network may seem counterintuitive. However, in practice, a conclusion is almost always drawn before its assumptions are fully articulated. It is useful, therefore, to question the assumptions underlying a conclusion, that is, to ask what assumptions are needed by a specific conclusion, given the stated facts.[22]

The conclusions of an argument network must further be related to one another. When the validity of conclusion A depends upon the validity of conclusion B, conclusion B may be said to be assumed by A. Hence, among the assumptions of a conclusion may be other necessary conclusions. In such a case, conclusions appear among another conclusion's outputs.

If one conclusion may thus be an output of another, the latter will further appear within the network as an input to the former. Such an input is termed here a *contingent*, that is, a conclusion that depends on another conclusion of interest. As we shall see, examining contingent and dependent conclusions enables us to probe an argument network, revealing the underlying structure. Formally, when two conclusions are related as in C2 $\rightarrow$ C1, this means that C1 is necessitated (assumed) by C2, and that C2 is contingent (dependent) upon C1.

Exhibit 12 summarizes and illustrates the architecture for argumentation. The basic form is a network of assertions amenable to Houdini processing. The assertions, located at the nodes, are labeled as facts, conclusions, and assumptions. Six facts (nodes that are inputs only), four conclusions (nodes with both inputs and outputs), and five assumptions (nodes that are outputs only) are related to each other in this example. Conclusion C2 is dependent upon both C1 and C3; C3 is dependent in turn upon C4. Hence, in this illustration, conclusion C2 rests upon the entire argumentative network.

With an argumentative architecture thus established, we can examine the bank position paper sequentially, one section of the paper at a time, to extract the principal assertions and enter them in slightly edited form into Houdini. This process establishes obvious relationships along the way. Examples of incorporated assertions are those illustrated in Exhibit 11.

Exhibit 12.
An Architecture for Argumentation

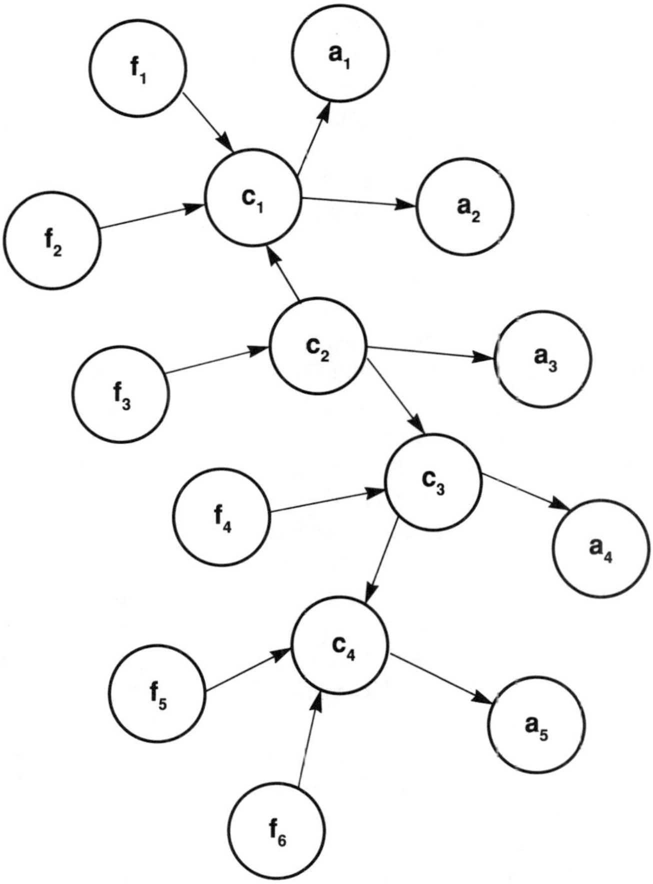

When this task is complete, we can begin to explore the resulting argument. A total of 71 assertions had been entered, connected by 88 relational links. We focus first on the structure, as opposed to the content, of the bank argument, as it had been abstracted and portrayed.

This technique identifies three characteristic problems with the formal structure of the argument: (1) unrelated assertions, that is, isolated assertions not employed elsewhere in the argument; (2) ill-formed conclusions, that is, conclusions not based on facts, or without stated assumptions; and (3) disconnected argument, that is, lack of connection among the conclusions of the argument as a whole.

The nature of these problems is illustrated in Exhibit 13, in which several links have been dropped from the properly constructed argument of Exhibit 12. Here, facts F1 and F3 are no longer drawn upon, and become unrelated assertions. Conclusion C2 is now ill-formed, because it employs no facts. And, conclusion C4 is disconnected from the balance of the argument.

These characteristic problems pervade the initial representation of the bank's argument. Eleven assertions are wholly unrelated to other assertions. Among apparent conclusions, only eight are not ill-formed. Among the well-formed conclusions, only three are connected, and upon inspection of the internal logic of these conclusions, none appears to be obviously justifiable.

In working with these problems it became apparent to me that the argument could be substantially tightened by locating implicit relationships among assertions distant from each other within the position paper. This I did, eventually extending the links among the assertions from 88 to 136. Still, the characteristic problems persisted.

Clearly, much of the argument of the bank's position paper had escaped rough attempts to capture it. Among the apparent reasons were the following: (1) loss of argument through abstraction of the original text; (2) loss of argument unstated, but implicit within the linear composition of the original text; (3) loss of argument known by the Bank, but not included in the position paper; and (4) loose reasoning within the original argument itself, for example, a low reliance on facts, a tendency to jump to conclusions, and a reluctance to acknowledge assumptions. Notably, only the last of these four reasons reflects upon the worthiness of the bank's original argument.

An analytic exercise like this would probably not be enough to evaluate an argument already presented in written form, as with the bank's position paper. It might, however, be a useful first step, where the argument might ultimately be completely reconstructed in consultation with those familiar with it. Though such a reconstruction is beyond the scope of the present work, it has much to recommend it, both as a means for assessing business value in the situation of interest, and for obtaining further insights into structured argumentation. For the same reasons it would also be worthwhile to develop an original position paper around a structured argument.

Exhibit 13.
Characteristic Problems in Argumentative Structure

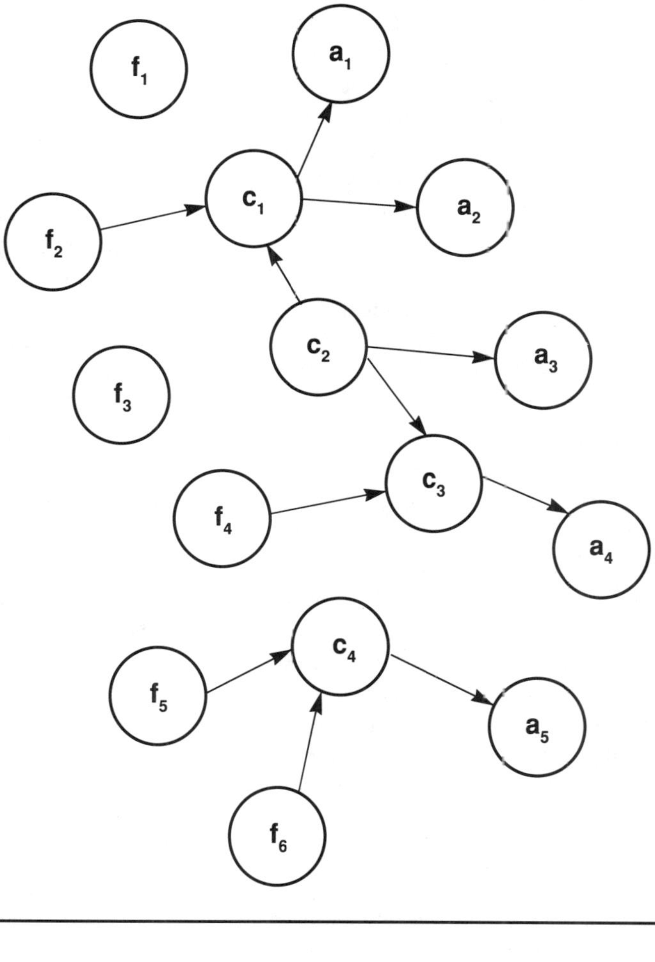

Conclusion

To measure the business value of information technologies in terms of putting a number on it in the conventional sense is problematic, as all but the most naive will agree. The resolution of this problem, both in principle and in practice, is based necessarily upon a persuasive, justificatory argument. In the absence of such an argument, measurements are essentially meaningless.

Argumentation is thus fundamental to measurement, and, for this reason, it is worthwhile to focus on argumentation itself as a means for assessing the business value of information technologies. This is not to suggest that argumentation be substituted for measurement; rather, the two should be integrated. Interestingly, the work of others in this book, which focuses on the more direct measurement of the business value of information technology, also suggests convergence.

Kauffman and Kriebel[23] rightly observe that measures of business value acquire coherence as the building blocks of an organization's strategy, and that a system of measures, not a single measure, should be employed within an established institutional framework for measuring and monitoring. Within such a framework, they propose and illustrate the use of Data Envelopment Analysis for assessing the productivity effects of IT deployment. Viewed in our terms, such assessment requires a careful and refined management argument, involving not only underlying economic theory, but data, assumptions, and conclusions particular to the situation faced by management.

Similarly, Strassmann[24] suggests a Return on Management approach to measuring the business value of IT. This approach derives practical meaning from both underlying theory and situational context, and can be used for comparative within-industry data analysis. Here again, a strategic management argument within an accepted institutional framework is the appropriate vehicle for conveying the meaning of the measurements.

Finally, Berger's[25] enterprise view also emphasizes the importance of management strategy in providing the context for the measures he proposes.

Traditionally, measurement has been considered a quantitative endeavor. Development of a management strategy and establishment of an institutional framework, on the other hand, are seen as essentially qualitative. The chief conclusion of this chapter is that measuring the business value of information technology necessarily involves both quantitative and qualitative considerations.

This conclusion defines the important task for management: to seek out a satisfactory balance between quantitative and qualitative factors when assessing the business value of information technologies. Neither the Mystique of Quantity nor the Mystique of Quality should be allowed to prevail. Rather, management should focus on the careful development and assessment of the crucial arguments it must consider.

Notes

1. The XYZ Bank is a fiction, although selected data have been drawn from actual sources for purposes of realistic illustration.
2. See especially Strassmann's discussion in this volume of current methods of information technology valuation. Measurements are controversial for good reasons. In this regard, see R.O. Mason, "The Role of Dialogue in the Measurement Process," in R.O. Mason and E.B. Swanson (eds.), *Measurement for Management Decision*, Addison-Wesley, Reading, Mass., 1981, pp. 519–527.
3. A. Kaplan, *The Conduct of Inquiry*, Chandler Publishing Company, San Francisco, 1964, p. 172. Kaplan also presents a full chapter on the philosophy of measurement.
4. See note 3 above, p. 206.
5. Note the theory necessary to support Strassmann's "return on management" measure, for example. See Strassmann, this volume.
6. C.W. Churchman, "Suggestive, Predictive, Decisive, and Systemic Measurements," in Mason and Swanson, 1981, pp. 74–80 (see note 2).
7. S. Toulmin, *The Uses of Argument*, Cambridge University Press, Cambridge, 1958, p. 11.
8. C. Spezzano, "Unconventional Outliners," *PC World*, March, 1986, pp. 168–175; W.R. Hershey, "Thinktank: An Outlining and Organizing Tool," *Byte Magazine*, May, 1984, pp. 189–194; and J. Conklin, "A Survey of Hypertext," Software Technology Program, MCC, Austin, Tex., October 1986.
9. Conklin (note 8) provides an excellent introduction to hypertext and discusses its applicability to argumentation.
10. T. Moran, "Enhancing Ideation," invited address, Interact '84, 1st IFIP Conference on Human-Computer Interaction, London, September 4–7, 1984; and F.G. Halasz, T.P. Moran, and R.H. Trigg, "Notecards in a Nutshell," Intelligent Systems Laboratory, Xerox Palo Alto Research Center, 1986.
11. B. Lutes-Schaab, R. McCall, Jr., W. Schuler, and H. Werner, "MIKROPLIS—A Textbank Management System and Idea Processor," Gesellschaft fuer Information und Dokumentation (GID), Frankfurt am Main, 1986. The original motivation for MIKROPLIS is the work on issue-based information systems (IBIS) undertaken by Rittel and colleagues in W. Kunz and H. Rittel, "Issues as Elements of Information Systems," DMG Occasional Paper No. One, Design Methods Group, January 1972.
12. Kandt's tool incorporates a number of interesting features beyond those mentioned here. K. Kandt, "A Tool to Support Competitive Argumentation," *Journal of Management Information Systems*, Vol. 3, No. 4, 1987, p. 62.
13. L. Applegate, T. Chen, B. Konsynski, and J. Nunamaker, "Knowledge Management in Organizational Planning," *Journal of Management Information Systems*, Vol. 3, No. 4, 1987, p. 25. See also L. Applegate, B. Konsynski, and J. Nunamaker, "A Group Decision Support System for Idea Generation and Issue Analysis in Organizational Planning," *Proceedings, Conference on Computer-Supported Cooperative Work*, Austin, Tex., December 3–5, 1986, pp. 16–34.
14. The application of strategic-assumption surfacing and analysis is based on the original work of Mason and is developed further in collaboration with Mitroff. R.O. Mason, "A Dialectical Approach to Strategic Planning," *Management Sci-*

ence, 13, 1969, B403–B414; I. Mitroff, R. Mason, and V. Barabba, "Policy as Argument—A Logic for Ill-Structured Decision Problems," *Management Science*, 28, 12, December 1982, pp. 1391–1404. For an overview of strategic tools see A.J. Rowe, R.O. Mason, and K.E. Dickel, *Strategic Management and Business Policy: A Methodological Approach*, Addison-Wesley, Reading, Mass., 1982.

15. See L.S. Richman, "Software Catches the Team Spirit," *Fortune*, June 8, 1987, pp. 125–136, which also describes the Colab effort.
16. G. Foster, "Colab: Tools for Computer-based Cooperative Work," Computers and Information Systems Colloquium, Graduate School of Management, University of California, Los Angeles, June 4, 1987, p. 39.
17. M. Stefik, G. Foster, D. Bobrow, K. Kahn, S. Lanning, and L. Suchman, "Beyond the Chalkboard: Computer Support for Collaboration and Problem Solving in Meetings," *Communications of the ACM*, 30, 1, January 1987, pp. 32–47.
18. See Conklin, note 8 above.
19. MaxThink, Inc., 230 Crocker Avenue, Piedmont, Cal. 94610.
20. The use of Houdini for this exploratory purpose should not be taken as a product endorsement. The author has made no systematic evaluation of Houdini.
21. The basic building blocks for argumentation are inspired in part by the work of Toulmin (note 7), as developed and applied by Mitroff (note 14).
22. This concept parallels the notion of assumption surfacing, as presented in support of strategic planning by Mason and since incorporated in other work, as described in note 14.
23. Kauffman and Kriebel, this volume.
24. Strassmann, this volume. See also Paul A. Strassmann, *Information Payoff*, The Free Press, New York, 1985.
25. Berger, this volume.

VI

Case Studies

As we might expect, different companies are taking different approaches to the measurement of IT's business value. This chapter presents three real-world case studies examining different frameworks for value measurement. The cases illustrate many issues and problems identified in the preceding chapters.

The first case, Mutual Benefit Life, presents a fairly common situation: the head of a line IS organization is called on to document business benefits from existing IT investments. The second case, American Standard, shows how an IS executive free of line responsibilities measures the value of existing and proposed IT investments. The final case shows how an outside consultant, in this case, Paul Berger, author of Chapter 3, works with a bank's IS head to identify value measures suited to that company. The bank asked that its identity not be disclosed.

Mutual Benefit Life Insurance Company

At Mutual Benefit Life, management traditionally regarded IT costs as part of corporate overhead expenses. A key measure of IT performance was IS's ability to tightly manage IS costs. To see how well IS was doing, management compared Mutual Benefit's IS costs against those of competitors. If these were roughly in line, IS was seen as doing a good job of managing costs.

According to Charles McCaig, Mutual Benefit's Senior Vice President for Information Services, this focus on IS costs has intensified over the past 10 years with the commoditization of insurance products, a result of industry deregulation. At that time the company found itself engaged in fierce price competition with a host of new rivals in its traditional markets: insurance and pension plans. Margins had fallen significantly and the company stepped up its examination of all operations costs. Senior management aimed at streamlining the company to become more cost competitive. In January 1986, a newly reorganized executive committee asked McCaig and his IS management team to document IS's contributions to the business. The specific question McCaig was called on to address was: How much can Mutual Benefit afford to spend on information services and keep its products competitive?

The executive committee that issued this challenge had two overriding concerns: cost control and competitive positioning. McCaig and his staff gathered data for a presentation that addressed both of these areas but treated each in a different way. Quantitative measures were used to establish that IS was an efficient operation and that its costs were under control, while qualitative and anecdotal data were used to assess IT's competitive impact. In the process McCaig and his staff were making a case for the value-added potential of information technologies.

Background

Founded in 1845, Mutual Benefit Life is a mutual insurance firm with headquarters in Newark, New Jersey. *Fortune* magazine ranks it as the 16th largest U.S. life insurance company, with $57 billion of life insurance in force, assets of $10.1 billion, and a return on invested assets of 10.04 percent. Mutual Benefit's chief product lines are in the areas of group life and health insurance, individual life insurance, and group pension plans. Its individual life insurance has traditionally been of the whole-life variety, though in recent years the company has introduced a successful universal-life product. It markets its products primarily through its nationwide network of career agents. As with most financial services companies, Mutual Benefit's business depends on the reliability and efficiency of its host computer systems.

Assessing Business Value of Information Technologies

In a July 1986 presentation to the senior management committee, McCaig focused on the business benefits from the company's existing information systems. His greatest success, he said, was in convincing top management that money spent on IS was building an asset that positions the company competitively. McCaig used measures of replacement cost and direct-labor substitution to convey the magnitude of this IT asset. He had figured that the IS department, with a $38 million budget, watches over an IT asset (computers, communications equipment, workstations, software, and databases) with a replacement value of approximately $500 million. Half of this investment is in databases, which McCaig estimated would take 800 people about 5 years to transfer from paper to electronic form.

McCaig illustrated IT's impact on the two critical business concerns identified by senior management: cost control and competitive positioning. On the subject of cost control, McCaig showed that IS efficiency was improving over time. Absolute IS budgets had remained flat for most of this decade while IS's productivity had grown dramatically over the period. In 1986 the department had 502 people doing 5 times the work performed by 735 people back in 1981. Other departments had also reduced their staffing requirements as a result of IS-engineered business systems. IS expenses as a percentage of company expenses had actually declined since 1981, from 17.2 percent to 16.3 percent. In addition, IS host computers handled 7 times as many transactions as they did in 1981. The cost of processing a claim dropped from $17 to $9, and turnarounds on claim processing decreased from 30 to 6 days, with error rates declining.

On the subject of competitive positioning, McCaig explained how IT had improved the effectiveness of Mutual Benefit's business activities, thereby helping the company competitively. The technology had reduced the cost of doing business; enhanced products, services, and business processes; and facilitated business change. Because these latter two benefits did not lend themselves to quantitative measures, McCaig chose to address them by focusing on examples of successful implementations.

According to McCaig, this valuation-by-example approach was quite effective, in no small part because it fit with a management culture that places business logic considerations on par with bottom-line measures. As he spoke to the executive committee, McCaig described several key Mutual Benefit products and services and equated the value of each IT system with its indispensability. He pointed out how difficult it would be to provide a particular product or service without the system. Here are some of McCaig's examples:

> *Adjustable Life.* The complex nature of this product, coupled with the monthly calculations frequency, requires a computer system to administer any reasonable volume of business. This is truly a computer-age product.
>
> *Customer Service Hot Line.* This approach to customer service provides a toll-free telephone number that enables policyholders and agents to ask questions about and make changes in their policies. This facility could not be provided, *at any cost,* without Alpha Index, STAR Individual, and LIFE/70 [host-based systems] which provide on-line access to policy data.
>
> *Medical Claims Systems.* Currently 55 medical claims per examiner per day are possible. It used to be about 20. We couldn't physically pay all medical claims and LTD claims without system support.

McCaig said the example-oriented approach went over well because it enabled business executives to see where each IT system fit, like pieces in a jigsaw puzzle, into Mutual Benefit's broader business strategies. It also gave top executives an "architectural" outlook on information-systems development. "Senior management learned the value of growing the IT asset laterally through continued applications and systems development," he said. "Without continued growth in systems architecture, it becomes increasingly harder and costlier to close the systems-development gap as business requirements change."

At the same time, valuation-by-example was consistent with IS's supporting role within the corporation. At Mutual Benefit IS is not a profit center; it functions purely in support of the user organizations (group life, group pension, etc.), each of which has its own business strategies. This valuation approach takes the user's business strategies as given and assesses an IT system by its ability to serve these strategies. Says McCaig, "My justification for any project is that the business people said it was worthwhile and served their purposes. They're the ones with the bottom-line payoff numbers."

American Standard, Inc.

Gary Biddle, Vice President of Management Information Services (MIS) at American Standard, oversees the company's diverse worldwide IT activities from his office in midtown Manhattan. His is primarily a staff position with responsibility for the corporate data utility and communications network. Biddle's principal responsibility is to direct MIS with policy and guidelines for American Standard's numerous strategic business units (SBUs) and joint ventures throughout North America, Western Europe, and the developing nations. He must establish this direction not only with an incisive view of IT's impact on the marketplace but also as a practitioner implementing technology in medium-size businesses, the SBUs.

Biddle and Michael Fischer, American Standard's Director of Information Management and Technology, are creating an environment in which the SBU's MIS organizations can be managed as businesses within a business. In the two years since Biddle, a company veteran, brought Fischer on board, the two have designed an integrated framework of business/technology models and processes. These models were designed to help MIS align its activities more closely with business objectives. In addition, Fischer, who has held key MIS positions with Raytheon and Martin Marietta and now explores strategic technologies for American Standard, says they are providing consultation to company executives on the potential expanded use of IT and its impact on the business.

"We will be successful," says Fischer, "when our general business managers feel they must give as high a priority to managing IT as they do to marketing, engineering, and manufacturing functions. This will require confidence in the tools and management methods we have developed. This confidence can best be obtained in the form of results."

Biddle and Fischer's four-stage IT-management methodology enables MIS and business managers to identify for any IT investment the key business objectives, measures, and performance targets. These quantitative business objectives would then drive the IT planning processes, helping managers decide which projects to fund, which to reject, which to expand, which to modify, and which to roll back or discontinue. The methodology is still very new and has only just begun to be applied in the business units. Biddle and Fischer freely admit that they have a considerable selling job ahead of them because the approach is more proactive than MIS people are used to, and because it addresses all forms of IT, strategic and tactical, whether managed by MIS or not.

Background

American Standard is a diversified manufacturer with 1987 sales of $3.3 billion. Its SBUs fall into three main categories: air-conditioning products, building products, and transportation products. The company and its affiliates manufacture in some two dozen countries and market in nearly every country in the world.

For the most part, American Standard is fielding mature product lines in mature markets. This requires a marketing reliance on replacement sales, premium products, and enhanced service offerings. The SBUs coordinate closely with suppliers, dealers, and customers for the information and flexibility crucial to maintaining or improving their market standing.

At American Standard, the New York-based parent corporation functions primarily as an overseer and financier to the SBUs. The SBUs are required to file an annual operating plan with headquarters. Most line functions, MIS included, have been decentralized within the business units.

Identifying Performance Measures for IT Investments

The vast reach of American Standard's business holdings has caused Biddle and Fischer to take a very global approach to IT management and measurement. Their approach, as shown in Exhibit 14, centers on an all-inclusive model of the IT architecture, considered along three dimensions. These dimensions are:

1. Processor: mainframe/corporate, functional/departmental, workstation/personal
2. Business portfolio: institutional, factory automation, professional support services, external support services
3. Standards: application, data, communications

This architectural model enables an MIS manager reviewing the existing IT systems to determine where each system fits within the total spectrum of IT capabilities and possibilities (for example, a computer-aided design and manufacturing system is a functional/department-level system, a factory-automation application, and a Manufacturing Automation Protocol-compat-

Exhibit 14.
Architectural Model for Computing

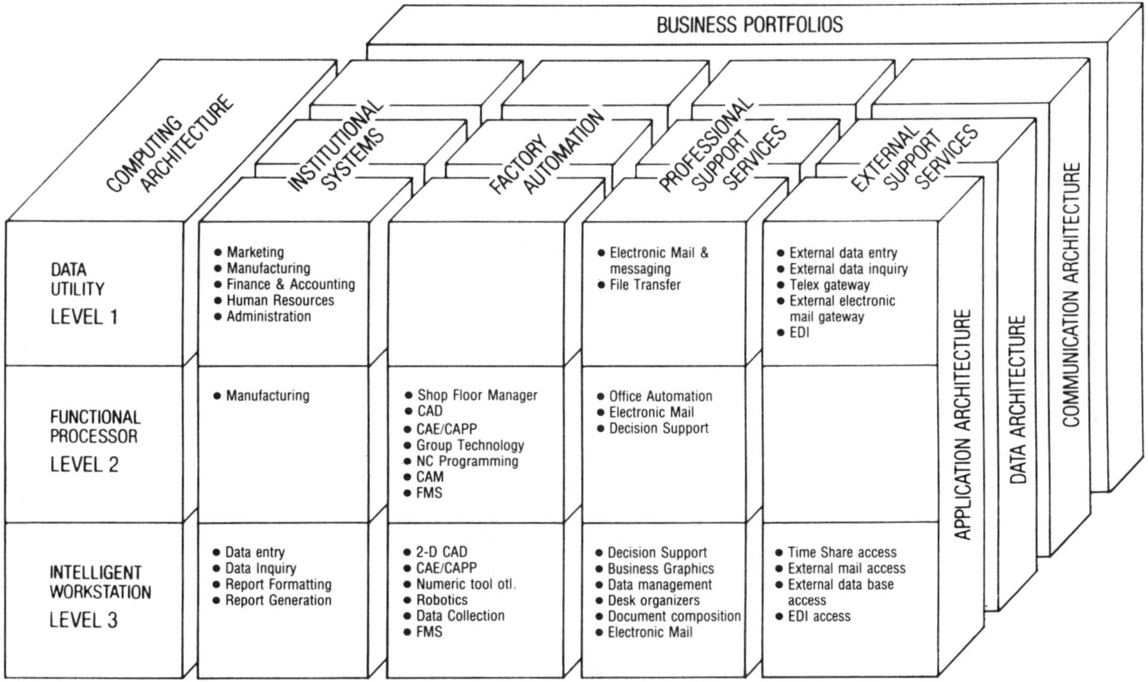

ible, token-bus, broadband local area network). The model would also allow MIS to explore the opportunity space of IT applications yet to be implemented, or to establish a technology direction (that is, a range of professional support services, such as financial modeling, currently supported by company mainframes, might be more efficiently and effectively furnished through microcomputer software).

With this architectural model as its centerpiece, the IT-management methodology then begins to evaluate IT investments in the context of broader business programs and projects (see Exhibit 15). The four stages of this methodology are:

1. Managing business strategy
2. Managing the investment
3. Managing the portfolio
4. Managing the benefits

The final stage, managing the benefits, is where business and MIS managers identify business measures and performance targets suited to IT investments, and then track investment performance in accordance with these criteria. But to arrive at this stage managers must first consider the investment as it relates to an SBU's enterprise-level business mission. Biddle and Fischer have designed processes, and are building PC-based support tools, to assist managers every step of the way.

Stage One: Managing Business Strategy. In this initial stage, the manager outlines business objectives to be served. The model begins by focusing on critical success factors and from these deriving a set of business strategies. Broadly categorized they are:

- To create competitive advantage
- To improve management effectiveness
- To improve productivity

These goals break down into more focused objectives that serve as the basis for specific measures of investment performance. For example, the goal "to create competitive advantage" might break down into the objectives "improve time to market," "differentiate products," "design new products," and "enhance product quality." These goals and objectives should also help managers establish priorities when reviewing IT investment proposals identified within the management process.

Stage Two: Managing the Investment. It is at this stage that managers begin to take stock of their in-place IT investments and explore new in-

Exhibit 15.
Information Management Planning Methodology

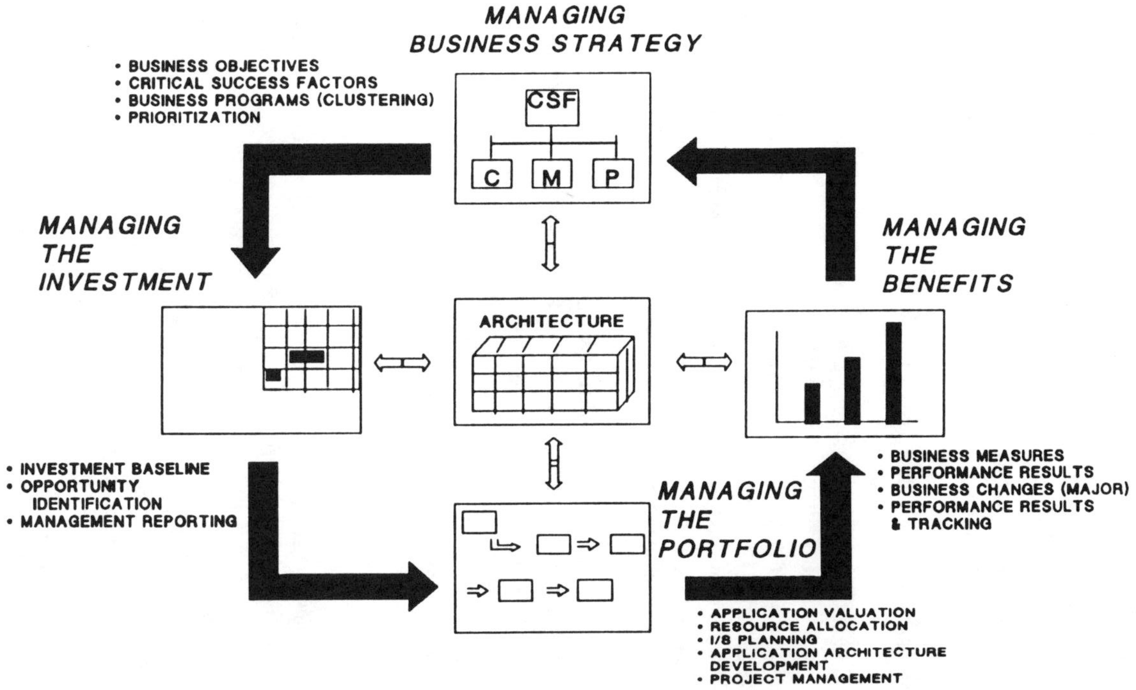

vestment opportunities. They engage in an investment-baselining exercise in which current IT expenditures are given dollar values and broken down according to cost components (operational, development, maintenance) and portfolio components, such as institutional systems, factory-automation systems, etc. The manager also develops an architectural profile of existing systems using the three-dimensional model discussed above. This baselining exercise, looking at the financial and architectural characteristics of the IT infrastructure, enables managers to assess current resource commitments to IT and the strategic positioning of the IT asset. It also serves as the platform for identifying new IT opportunities.

Stage Three: Managing the Portfolio. Here is where the link between enterprise-level business planning and MIS planning is made most explicit. Managers are given a framework for assessing new IT investment proposals and for determining how to allocate resources between a portfolio of new and existing systems. The enterprise-level goals and objectives identified in Stage One come into play. Senior executives and MIS managers work together to plan new business programs to address business objectives and take advantage of opportunities in the marketplace. These new business programs incorporate the strategic IT projects identified in Stage Two. Existing IT systems are also judged by whether they fit into broader business responses to marketplace challenges.

Biddle and Fischer have also developed a tactical approach to managing the existing portfolio of applications. For each application, users rate functional quality (that is, ease of use) and functional coverage. The MIS people rate technical quality. Ratings of both groups are on scales of 0 to 100 with 100 the best score. Each application is then plotted as a circle in a two-dimensional box chart, with one axis representing the user rating and the other representing MIS's evaluation (see Exhibit 16, "Information Technology Application Valuation"). The diameter of each application's circle varies proportionately with the amount of money spent maintaining that application. This bubble chart helps MIS managers distinguish the applications that are doing well (those that users and technical people both rate highly) from those needing enhancement (high technical, low user), refurbishment (low technical, high user), and replacement (low technical, low user). It also tells MIS whether maintenance money is being spent effectively. Maintenance funds, the big bubbles, should be concentrated in the enhancement and refurbishment quadrants, since neither high technical/high user nor low technical/low user applications warrant much maintenance.

Stage Four: Managing the Benefits. In the final stage, the methodology selects specific business measures and performance targets for strategic IT

Exhibit 16.
Information Technology Application Valuation
Business Unit Report by Functional Area
Finance & Accounting

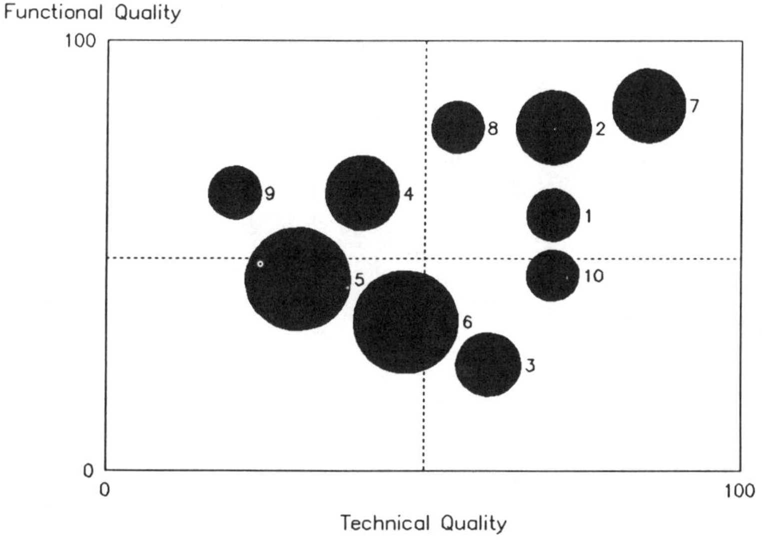

Legend

Costs (000's)

	Prod.	Maint.	% Cov.
1. Credit/AR	$75	$ 13	85%
2. Invoicing	$20	$ 26	100%
3. Payroll	$45	$ 26	82%
4. Accounts Payable	$30	$ 26	82%
5. Sales & Comm	$30	$ 52	60%
6. Cost Accounting	$45	$ 52	75%
7. General Ledger	$150	$ 26	91%
8. Human Resources	$10	$ 13	85%
9. Capital Budget	$ 5	$ 13	80%
10. Fixed Assets	$10	$ 13	82%

198_ Maintenance Costs
½ inch bubble—$50,000
Legend in Priority Sequence

investments identified in Stage Three. Two different categories of measures of IT-system value-added are presented: (1) criteria for justifying proposed new investments, and (2) criteria for tracking existing investments over time. The first category of measures ties a new investment decision directly to SBU goals and objectives, while the second translates these business-driven considerations into hard, observable quantities.

1. Criteria for justifying proposed new investments (justification measures): A unitary "cumulative index" is created for each proposed IT investment. This index is computed through a speculative assessment of the impact of an IT investment on the enterprise's various critical success factors. Numerical values and weights are assigned to the various critical success factors as well as to the impacts (high, medium, low). The cumulative index is placed alongside a timeline that represents the expected implementation lead time on the proposed investment. A breakdown of expected costs, capital, and expense, is also presented. This approach allows managers to assess the trade-off between a new investment's strategic payoff, its lead time, and its cost.
2. Criteria for tracking existing investments over time (tracking measures): Enterprise-level objectives serve as the basis for selecting quantitative performance measures and targets. For example, a CAD/CAM system may have been justified on the grounds that it promoted the goal of "creating competitive advantage" by "differentiating products," "designing new products," and "enhancing product quality." The CAD/CAM investment performance, then, could be tracked by measuring the number and variety of new products introduced, the resulting increase in market share, the reduction of marketing and engineering lead times, and the decline in warranty claims. These numerical measures can be compared to targets set by senior management.

Biddle and Fischer maintain that the purpose of this four-part methodology is to encourage managers at American Standard to identify IT-investment performance measures right up front, rather than after the fact, as often happens. The methodology also serves as a platform for management action. In the initial round of decision-making, when the business case for a new investment is being argued, managers rely primarily on the first category of measures: the justification measures, such as the cumulative index, the timeline, and the cost profile. In subsequent rounds, after an investment has been made and implemented, the second category of measures—the tracking measures—swings into action. These hard, observable metrics tell managers whether an IT investment is living up to the promise depicted for it by the original business-case justification.

Conclusion

According to Fischer, this approach roughly maps into the existing management decision-making process at American Standard. Initial IT-investment decision-making involves managers who are making a leap of faith in justifying new technology such as CAD/CAM. The re-investment process finds these same managers requiring quantitative, hard-dollar measures, and documentation of the actual business payoff from the in-place system. In this re-investment process, decisions are made either to maintain the existing level of funding, to expand the investment, to modify it, or to roll it back.

Biddle and Fischer recognize that their challenge is to gain acceptance among general managers for the inclusion of IT, alongside other business functions, in the strategic planning process.

Case Study of a Bank

The senior IS Vice President of a large Northeastern retail bank says the company continues to justify many IT investments largely on the basis of operational measures: projected cost reductions or cost avoidance. This approach contrasts, he remarks, with the company's push in recent years toward using IT for strategic purposes. Since 1985, the bank has been using a central customer-relationship database to support a relationship-oriented, rather than product-oriented, market strategy.

The senior IS VP and the Director of Planning met with Paul Berger, author of Chapter 3, to assess the IT value measures currently in use at the bank. The purposes of the meeting were to review the bank's current IT activities, and to use them as the basis for applying the methodology described in Berger's chapter.

Berger's methodology was applied as follows:

- Review the company's overall business strategies
- Review company strategies for the use of IT
- Categorize existing IT activities according to whether they represent internal/operational, strategic/competitive, or product/service activities
- Review the measurements currently used for these IT activities
- Match IT activities with corporate business strategies and IT strategies
- Determine appropriate measures for IT activities, based on categorization and matching exercises

For purposes of this case study, a select group of IT systems in place at the bank was examined. This group consisted of several systems put in place since 1985 to support the bank's relationship-based market strategy. The bank already has very well-defined business and IT strategies, so the exercise of matching IT activities to strategies was fairly straightforward.

Background

This major retail bank, with more than 200 branches, belongs to a holding company whose other divisions engage in corporate lending, international lending, investment banking, merchant banking, securities trading, institutional asset management, letters of credit, and foreign-currency trading. The retail bank is one of the top depository institutions in its metropolitan area. Its products and services address the consumer and small-to-midsized commercial markets. Its financial assets are primarily in the form of commercial loans, consumer loans, revolving credit, mortgage loans, lease financing, and home equity loans. The bank also generates revenue from consumer credit-card fees, account service charges, merchant credit-card processing, automated-teller-machine banking, private banking, electronic cash management, trust and estate management, personal custody, portfolio management, discount brokerage, private placements, interest-rate caps, swaps, leveraged buyouts, and employee stock-ownership plans. Depository products include checking, investment checking, savings, money market, CD, and IRA accounts. The bank's parent is in the process of acquiring two large out-of-state retail banks.

The bank began its push toward relationship-oriented banking in 1984, at the behest of the head of the consumer banking group. This new thrust came in response to changes in the bank's competitive environment—specifically, the successes of banking giant Citibank and two nonbanks, Merrill Lynch and Fidelity Investments, with relationship-oriented market strategies. A relationship-oriented approach segments the customer base into demographic categories and develops specialized products and services to address the needs of each category; the bank's former approach, product-oriented, involved marketing generalized products and services across all customer segments. The bank has already realigned its operations to serve four distinct relationship categories: affluent customers, middle-income customers, students, and low-income customers.

The bank's corporate parent has identified retail banking and consumer lending as a major growth area and IT as central to its retail market strategy. Prior to its move to relationship-oriented banking, the bank's IT activities focused heavily on back-office applications. Since that time it has taken great strides to improve its interface with and to enhance service to the general public. It has established a staff-level quality-of-service monitoring department, installed a customer-service hot line, created integrated account-balance statements, and allowed customers to link accounts so that fees, charges, and privileges are based on the current status of all their accounts.

Supporting this relationship-banking strategy are six key information systems, all brought on-line since 1985. They include:

- A centralized customer database, giving the current status of each customer's accounts with the bank.
- A central pricing and statementing system that interfaces with the bank's various application systems, calculates fees and service charges based on linked-account activity, and produces unified account-balance statements for each customer-relationship category.
- A branch-automation system that accesses the central customer-account database, displays data on current product/service information and competitors' offerings, performs what-if scenarios and projections on various accounts, and speeds up the opening and closing of accounts.
- A teller-automation system that accesses the central customer-account database, updates transaction information promptly, and produces an audit trail of transactions by teller.
- A customer-service automation system that pulls current data from other bank information systems and delivers it to an on-line human service representative or, by synthesized voice response, directly to an incoming caller.
- A back-office decision support system, built upon a relational database, that enables line and branch-office managers to monitor operational performance in real-time and to map out market strategies.

Selecting Appropriate IT Performance Measures

The bank's IT strategy to date had primarily addressed four of the organization's business objectives: relationship-oriented marketing, service enhancement, delivery restructuring, and internal control. The next step in the analysis was to determine how closely the existing IT activities matched the objectives. In keeping with Berger's methodology, this required a rough categorization of IT activities according to nature of impact:

- Category One: internal/operational
- Category Two: strategic/competitive
- Category Three: product/service

After the matching and categorizing exercises were performed, appropriate IT-value measures were identified. The findings of the study were as follows:

- The centralized customer database could be classified only as an internal/ operational system (Category One), since it entails no direct interface with customers and is not sold externally as a product or service. The database is both a foundation and a springboard for further development of strategic/competitive (Category Two) and product/service (Category Three) information systems. The database is a central component in an IT infrastructure enabling the bank to carry out its relationship-oriented market strategy. The information it contains crosses all bank activities and feeds into the other five key applications. The database provides indirect, but indispensable, support to the bank's relationship-oriented market strategy, service-enhancement strategy, and delivery-restructuring strategy. As an infrastructure component, its value cannot be measured in terms of direct revenue-generating impacts, but it can be treated as an IT "asset," according to Berger's definition. This would enable the bank to amortize the value of the database over its useful life and to charge the various business activities that benefit from it. In this way the database's economic value can be reflected in the bank's costs of production and the prices it charges its customers.

- The central pricing and statementing system could be classified only as a strategic/competitive system (Category Two), because it controls a significant element of the customer interface: the integrated account-balance statement. The system provides direct support to the relationship-oriented market strategy and the service-enhancement strategy. Because it is strategic/competitive, its bottom-line value can be assessed. The measures are expanded loan sales, increased deposits, higher market share, more products per customer, and reduced customer attrition rate. As part of the organization's IT infrastructure the system can also be viewed as an IT asset. It will serve as the base enabling system for the newly acquired out-of-state banks.
- The branch-automation system could be classified as both internal/operational (Category One) and strategic/competitive (Category Two). As an internal/operational system, it provides value by increasing the productivity of branch sales and customer-service representatives, reducing the amount of paper to be processed, and controlling operational costs. These internal benefits directly contribute to the bank's objective of improving controls over operations. As a strategic/competitive system, the system provides value by freeing up employees' time for active selling, improving the quality of available product/service information and customer-account data, speeding up the opening and closing of accounts, heightening the perceived professionalism of bank staff, and generally enhancing customer service. Consequently, the system provides value by directly advancing the relationship-oriented market strategy, the service-enhancement strategy, and the delivery-restructuring strategy.

  The internal/operational system's impacts can be measured in terms of increased time spent on sales and marketing, improved account-processing throughput, reduced information-search time, and reduced administrative and paper-handling costs. The strategic/competitive impacts can be measured in terms of increases in number of new deposit accounts per branch and employee, increases in loan sales per branch and employee, and increases in number of customer inquiries served per branch and employee. Qualitative measures of customer satisfaction can also be performed.

- The teller-automation system could be classified only as internal/operational (Category One). It provides value by improving teller productivity, producing an audit trail of transactions by teller, and reducing the ability of customers to defraud the bank by drawing more than once against the same balance. Consequently, it directly contributes to the objective of controlling operations. Its value can be measured in terms of cost reduction and avoidance.
- The customer-service automation system could be classified as both internal/operational (Category One) and strategic/competitive (Category Two). Internally, it controls costs by moving customer-service inquiries out of the branch offices, and enhances service-representative productivity by automatically pulling information out of company databases. Consequently, it directly contributes to the operational-control strategy. Strategically, it improves on-line service representatives' ability to handle customer inquiries and interfaces directly with the public via voice response. Hence, it contributes directly to the relationship-oriented market strategy, the service-enhancement strategy, and the delivery-restructuring strategy. The internal/operational impact can be measured in terms of cost displacement by moving customer inquiries out of branch offices. The strategic/competitive impact can be measured in terms of increases in throughput of inquiries handled and accounts/transactions processed per representative per day—measures of increased customer activity. Qualitative measures of customer satisfaction can also be employed.
- The back-office decision support system is purely internal/operational (Category One). It promises to improve the quality and timeliness of operational performance data available to line and branch-office managers. Its initial justification was as a cost-saver, bringing in-house some analytical activities that had been farmed out to third-party firms. Consequently, the DSS directly serves the company's operational-control strategy. In addition, the system enables managers to evaluate the profitability of serving particular customers and niches, and of pursuing various marketing and service strategies. This internal/operational system can be evaluated in terms of cost displacement from satisfying existing ad hoc reporting requirements in-house. It can also be measured in terms of cost avoidance from satisfying unforeseen future ad hoc reporting requirements in-house, rather than going through a service bureau. The indirect future impacts of a superior decision support system on bank assets and deposits cannot

be calculated, since these impacts depend on management's ability and readiness to apply system-supplied information to business problems. Perhaps such business impacts can be measured by the most qualitative of techniques: by cataloguing examples of opportunities seized and threats averted thanks to the decision support system.

Conclusion

The IT business-value measures identified can serve the bank in two capacities: as criteria for justifying investments up-front, or as indicators for tracking and documenting benefits from systems already in place. The bank might also be able to use these measures to justify enhancements and upgrades to systems currently in place.

Paul Berger and James Kobielus, who represented ICIT and gathered the data for this case, wish to thank the bank for allowing ICIT to use their organization as a test case.

VIII

Conclusion

Measurement is an integral part of the management process. Without solid and acceptable measures of IT's business value, business people have no way of determining whether or not an IT strategy is actually helping their companies.

An examination of modern companies shows management using a number of measures to justify various potential investments and to assess the real business performance of existing investments. Consistent with this view, a chief conclusion of this book is that real-world business environments require multiple measures of IT's business value. A single measurement will not suffice.

Take the case of Johnson, the archetypal CEO whose drive for strategic IT hinged on management's ability to identify suitable performance measures for IT investments: measures that indicated whether an investment was truly bringing value to the enterprise. His drive was a success, in large part because management selected a variety of measures suited to the nature and impact of particular IT implementations. Time-series data of management value-added had established a general correlation between introduction of office technologies—desktop computing, executive information systems, voice mail—and management productivity. These technologies had also been linked to a measurable drop in marketing lead times, while CAD/CAM had improved engineering lead times. The firm was able to document some cost savings attributable to purely internal systems such as payroll, order-entry, and billing systems, but identified considerable room for improvement in these areas. Finally, an in-depth study of the firm's Midwestern POS implementation had identified factors contributing to the success or failure of this technology in various retail locations. Results from this study had convinced senior management that limited local or regional POS implementations were preferable to a full-scale nationwide rollout.

Johnson had worked closely with the Vice Presidents of Finance and of IS to establish a measurement framework that was acceptable to senior management and appropriate to the firm's business goals and competitive situation. The framework enabled managers to determine which existing IT investments have been successful, which should be modified and how, and which should be discontinued. This action-oriented measurement approach gave senior executives the tools to explore new strategic directions in IT.

The challenge for real-world managers is to select suitable measures. The selection of a measure depends on such things as:

- The purpose of the measurement;
- The nature of the activity being measured;
- The traditions and culture of the company;
- The style of top executives; and

- The requirements of significant outsiders, such as shareholders, banks, fund managers, investment analysts, government agencies, etc.

This book contains a mosaic of innovative and useful measurement approaches. Let us summarize the main points:

- Paul A. Strassmann's main point is that IT serves primarily to help management do its job. Therefore, he proposes as a measure of IT business value the Return-on-Management metric, a tool for measuring management productivity.
- Paul Berger's central theses are threefold. First, companies should use measures that are familiar to management. Second, managers can select suitable measures by categorizing IT investments according to impact (that is, internal/operational, strategic/competitive, product/service) and matching them against enterprise-level business strategy. Third, IT activity, including software and database construction, builds a company's technological infrastructure; thus it should be treated as an asset and amortized.
- Robert J. Kauffman and Charles H. Kriebel present a diagnostic model called Data Envelopment Analysis (DEA), which can be applied to IT implementations where there are multiple inputs and outputs and the precise interaction among them is not fully understood. They use DEA to assess the performance of one such implementation: a complex ATM network. The model is management-action oriented in that it helps managers to quantify IT implementation strategies and match them with management objectives.
- E. Burton Swanson states that a well-formed business case is essential to the proper determination of the business value of an IT proposal. He proposes that the textual parts of a proposal for company action be evaluated on equal terms with the quantitative portions. He identifies the textual portion of a business case as a form of argumentation and proposes that the quality and strength of the argumentation be enhanced by using idea-processing software.

Two of the real-world case studies demonstrate how selecting a measurement approach depends on the circumstances of the firm and the manager. The Mutual Benefit Life case shows how one IS head in an enterprise concerned primarily with cost control analyzed and established IT's business value in response to a senior management request. The American Standard case shows how a corporate staff-level IS head has developed IT measurement models and processes to encourage the evaluation of strategic IT investment in decentralized business units.

In the third real-world case, a bank IS executive works with ICIT's research team to select performance measures by applying Paul Berger's categorization approach.

The book now comes full circle, returning to the question posed at the outset:

- How can business executives tell good IT investments from bad ones?

The answer, of course, depends on valid and reliable measures of IT business value. For business and IS managers, the following action points will help them develop just such measures:

- Make information technology an important part of company strategy to accomplish major business objectives.
- Make sure that IT investments match company business strategy for IT use.
- Treat staff productivity and information technology as variables in the long-term planning model.
- Recognize that investments in infrastructure, including software and data, must be treated as long-term investments for measurement purposes.
- Apply IT to develop both the quantitative and the textual parts of a business case.
- Differentiate between business-performance measurements and measurements of IS department performance.
- Select appropriate business measures to implement management's vision for IT activities.

Investments in information technologies, in both the private and public sectors, will continue to grow. Many of these investment decisions will continue to be made on "gut feel." However, given the right planning and management tools, business executives can develop more rational, well-supported measurements of the business value of any IT strategy or implementation.

This book, presenting the results of the ICIT research team, is a source of practical ideas for the rational evaluation of IT investments. The bottom line for management is knowledge leading to effective action. For managers, measuring the business value of information technology means knowing whether the company's money is well-spent.

Index

Quick Reference of Key Concepts

The following list organizes index entries under seven key conceptual headings. These headings make up the "conceptual framework," as it were, of this book. Alphabetically, the seven headings are:

- Corporate functions and departments
- Costs
- Industries
- Information technologies
- Measures
- Performance
- Value

This reference of index entries allows the inquisitive reader to quickly determine the domain and range of discussion in the foregoing chapters.

T

U

V

W

X

Y

About the Authors

Paul A. Strassmann, president of Strassmann, Inc., is a recognized expert on information systems productivity. He is the author of *Information Payoff—The Transformation of Work in the Electronic Age* (Free Press, 1985). Before forming his own firm, Mr. Strassmann was vice president of systems applications for the Systems Group of Xerox Corporation. Prior to that Mr. Strassmann served as chief information systems executive, first for the General Foods Corporation and later for the Kraft Corporation.

Paul Berger is president of Paul Berger Consulting, Inc. Prior to forming his own firm, Mr. Berger was director, Strategic Information Systems, in the Corporate Information Systems department of RCA Corporation. Prior to joining RCA, he was a member of the automatic programming research group at the Sperry Rand Corporation that reported to Dr. Grace M. Hooper. Mr. Berger is currently president of the Society for Information Management (SIM).

Charles H. Kriebel is professor of Industrial Administration at Carnegie-Mellon University. He has also taught at the University of Pennsylvania and at MIT. Dr. Kriebel has authored more than 70 articles and reports in the areas of management science, computers and information systems, operations management, and applied economics.

E. Burton Swanson is associate professor of Information Systems at the Graduate School of Management, University of California, Los Angeles. His previous working associations include 10 years with IBM—primarily in computer application system development—and two years as a visiting scientist with the Studiengruppe fuer Systemforschung, Heidelberg, Federal Republic of Germany. Dr. Swanson is co-author of *Measurement for Management Decision* (with R.O. Mason), Addison-Wesley, 1981, and *Software Maintenance Management* (with B.P. Lientz), Addison-Wesley, 1980.

Robert J. Kauffman is an instructor of Information Systems, Graduate School of Business Administration, New York University. In May 1988, he received his Ph.D. in industrial administration from the Graduate School of Industrial Administration, Carnegie-Mellon University. Prior to completing his graduate studies, Dr. Kauffman worked in the finance industry.